SWOLE

FUTUREPOEM BOOKS
NEW YORK CITY
2018

SWOLE
Jerika Marchan

first edition | first printing

This edition first published in paperback by Futurepoem books
P.O. Box 7687 JAF Station, NY, NY 10116
www.futurepoem.com

Executive Editor: Dan Machlin
Managing Editor: Carly Dashiell
Assistant Editor: Ariel Yelen
Books Editor: Ted Dodson
Open Reading Period Managing Editor: Jennifer Tamayo

Guest Editors: Mei-mei Berssenbrugge and Roberto Tejada

Cover and interior design: Everything Studio (www.everythingstudio.com)
Copyediting: Carly Dashiell
Printed in the United States of America on acid-free paper

This project is supported in part by the New York State Council on the Arts with
the support of Governor Andrew Cuomo and the New York State Legislature.
It is also supported in part by public funds from the New York City Department
of Cultural Affairs in partnership with the City Council, as well as by The New
York Community Trust Harris Shapiro Fund, The Leaves of Grass Fund, and
Futurepoem's Individual Donors, Subscribers, and Readers. Futurepoem books
is the publishing program of Futurepoem, Inc., a New York state-based 501(c)3
non-profit organization dedicated to creating a greater public awareness and
appreciation of innovative literature.

Distributed to the trade by Small Press Distribution, Berkeley, California
Toll-free number (U.S. only): 800.869.7553
Bay Area/International: 510.524.1668
orders@spdbooks.org
www.spdbooks.org

[The story survived upstream of me]

This, the river bloated
turned outward on itself

       // a break through wide
a more natural state. Forget
the walls, the artificial banks
setting a thin route south
into the Gulf.

River found its mouth lacking
made itself big
to accommodate the surge.

Water, by volume
Water, by the ton, for miles
fills its container —
won't be kept out.

edge of a noise went further —
swept the surface gouged
out a state to spit you
into — a soppy, gray task

hot season bit out
the basic thinness of
late petals, stripped
ever newflesh, even
late summer   upbloom,   sunup

the diamonds in a terrible
                    diamonz waz terribl!!

                    you shoulda seen the sun!

                    up inna
                    a blizzard of 'em!
                    a blizzt waz here!
                    horrbl   all the water

                    an' then the SUN GONE

our collective dire thing met with
a bridge — a gap toward

quietquiet
quiet we wanderin' cuz
the lostness of it

            not   yet impermeable
            not   yet
            not   yet

            TV   solid
            RADIO   tight
            INTERNET   resistant
            ALL OVER   haze
            AIRWAVE
            STATIC
            what I saw

            call the government

// get you out of this

phone don't work

call the government!

don't   even   make   no sound

// get you out of this

///
    and a woman I could see
    sweat stains on her back
    was the heat
    a definite struggle with

what   corroded
                  swept

        away

left nothing undisturbed

    we were used to
    breathing in this
    almost ocean of air

    tongue   numb
    corpse   mouth
    poison   mouth
    fat tongue — all the biting
    could not make you slimmer —

// get you out of this

dismantle the bloat

the water

/ / /

///

[River, your kindly undulating mouth]

> *shake my head shake my head*
> *ain't nobody got time …*

Greetings from here

where are you

where you are

///

///

[FLATLAND BASIC RISING]

never, or hardly
none that I could see

what   circumference
hazard   this?

wind.   a fail jetstream.
fickle barometric

mess.   so, pressure.
p r e s s

coldfront watching me.

///

// often sickly, it's the way you move
against the lamplight —
the shadow, your stain against this wall —
it holds you.
your shadow cradles you to the bed.

your shadow cradles you,
a nest for its bird. //

FUCK THAT NOISE //
// tame that noise

often quickly, something ended —

the blitz.

o b l i t e r a t e d

e v a p o u r

// I told her
baby, we wanna get somewhere
we gonna have a lot

no shame. no more
of this twisting inside
to hide where we come from.

Where we stay at gonna be fine.
It's the getting-to. It's always hard. //

13

/ / /

[you don't want to know
where I come from]

If I said the dust from my window
was all the dust from my skin
would that gross you?

Look and look how visible I am
even all my things wear me.

/ / /

[*Tips & Tricks*]

- *Don't go out alone at night*
- *Don't wear clothing that is EZ 2 Remove*
- *The elbow is the strongest point on ur body.*
- *Go on the Pill*
- *Carry ur keys btwn ur knuckles*
- *Carry an umbrella*
- *Check under ur car & in the backseat*
- *If U! R in trouble, Scream, Yell for Help or Yell "Fire!"*
- *If U! R thrown into the trunk of a car: kick out the back taillight & start WAVING LIKE CRAZY*
- *If a robber! asks 4 ur wallet, toss it AWAY from U & RUN LIKE MAD N THE OTHER DIRECTION!*
- *IT IS ALWAYS BETTER 2 B SAFE THEN SORRY & BETTER PARANOID THEN DEAD*
- *As Women, we R always trying 2 B sympathetic: STOP IT! It may get you raped or worse killed*
- *THIS HAS SAVED LIVES*

Foundation's always uneven
Always will be. Can't afford to fix it.
We don't have the money, honey.

/ / /

[This is why we can't have nice things]

// A double-barrel shotgun is a semi-detached
house, so — symmetrical, sharing a central wall.
Usually raised two to three feet off the ground
could be built using fewer materials
and use less land per occupant:
ideal for poor people.

Rooms arranged follow each other
one behind another
living room bedroom bed room kitchen
often times with no closing doors
bathroom addition if you're lucky. //

// Northshore shotguns, named for
the north shore of Lake Pontchartrain,
were designed as summer houses for wealthy
whites and feature wide, wrap-around verandas. //

// *never quite straight or in a good line*
but beauty —
        still how she keeps correcting herself
        still keeps adding on even when things fall apart —
hanging by her own rust chipping away

// Chris says New Orleans has a love affair with itself — obsessed with its own quirks and too aware of its flaws to risk even polite detachment. *The most self-referential city. Its "charm". "You're only really welcome here if you decide to stay and even then — you're either local or you're not." ///*

///
[How can this mean nothing to you?]

gentle, slopheap

gentle.

I have not lived yet
in so tight a place

and mama
couldn't hold me.
I didn't want it.

but how terrific that my lung
has lunged —

lung'd

lung-ed

finally.

ain't never been
not happy — I been grateful —
ain't never been
not anything
blaze me

17

fire.
fire.
fire, *you're real.*

Gentle Slopheap,

I can't see where the bridge goes —

the light is all the way on the other side.

/ / /

///

I drove as you slept with your forehead heat
flushed against the glass. Radio off.
Highways west found us some calm
land flattened more and became clean—
our last-minute evacuation to Dallas,
land of swimming pools, to save us.

///

what's it culled

what   culled

what is held

can be

brightened

insistent foil

h e a v e

what beauty

had   lush

a lush perimeter

surround me

///

*// BRRRRRRRRRRRRRRRRRRRING!
BRRRRRRRRRRRRRRRIIIIIIIIIIIINNNNNGGGGGGG! //*

19

// BRRRRRRROOOOOMMMGGGG!!!

DA NEWZ WENT CORRUPTION
MUTE

MUTE

WHO WILL GIV IT 2 UZ?

MUTE. MUTE.
E - Z B U T T O N //

///
i dreamt the sand filled in
between my legs & the room
became a wasteland

lay tatter the drapery frame
the picture all different
& the girl inside —
her legs smooth
even the scars old
skinned-over extra tender
puffy flesh magnificent

shiny little hill of skin
///

- ▫ *Water – at least a gallon per person per day*
- ▫ *Food – include non-perishables*
- ▫ *A non-electric can opener*
- ▫ *First aid kit and prescription drugs*
- ▫ *Flashlight*
- ▫ *Cell phones*
- ▫ *Cash*
- ▫ *Keys*
- ▫ *Contact information for family and emergency services*
- ▫ *Insurance papers, medical records, medications lists, the deed*
  or lease to your home, bank account numbers, social security
  cards, passports, birth certificates. Keep in a waterproof container.

/ / /

[Run, fast.]

summer held you like a choking baby

//something strained.
should I?   only
know how to ask

mea culpa.
o

— everything mistaken —
is hazardous air —
is not finite —
is so much grosser —
is listed down on stone —

but pray for me anyway

beat your chest

mea culpa

Noah's wife — if she feared anything at all
was it the flood
or all the animals? //

summer tried suffocating you
like a baby in a grocery bag.

// [timing]

the road is an oilslick

getting somewhere //

// when the sea bucked wildly with you in it
how tried you, strong fingers
— *I'd never seen such* — grappled
with the sea, enraged the water
slipped through your hands —
like it was something you could conquer //

blasted.

// when closely — when closer
tightened —

a lightstorm.

I see the edges lift off the road.
I pastel like a baby. //

///

Y'all, Imma blank one.

Blank one steel

up

steel

up

shore

when I press my
press   up my

inside   my

inside of upness   turned

          ragged turned brained
sed

sed, *girl*
be vulnerable

fuck that big word.

that big fuckin' word.

"vuln'rubl"

When I see you with the lights
crossed out, I wanna sing. I wanna
sing into my skin all day & let it bounce
off the wallpaper & let it be loud

enough to peel the wallpaper
with my hands. with
my hands & with my hands

I break inside from the
self, I was blasted
little muttering said

Be the bayonet. I'll be the wound.
Be the bayonet. I'll be the wound.

/ / /

///

when i brim
i brim up to you
aghast the noise
brim quiet brim
you led to
the tip of
a ledge
a grove
an edge
a fire.

set me squander
overmeats she eats
us under—
the safe place
a squall
there a bridge
stretch here
the bend made

deep. equal eye
sore to spread me
over a fire
a fire fire fire

basic and weary
the way you spread
the meats for me
               ///

feels like we're not having a conversation

nah, you're not even listening

[HOW EVERYONE SHINES IN THIS CITY]

// [maggot-breathed, she was so sweet it all]

THANK YOU THANK YOU THANK YOU

y'all pushpin heart don't burn
as good as you think

JESUS JESUS JESUS   ain't the pavement always uneven—
ever to ever find your feet
where they need to be //

THANK YOU
THANK YOU
THANK YOU

JESUS   JESUS   JESUS

              Sunday evening
after the rain has left my room coldish
aftermath   window open, I light
candles —   makes   me   feel
oceanic   or just salty
and I pair up my socks for the week.

So far, I have measured my life
in paper cuts and mishandled lectures.
I place importance on things that can be folded symmetrically.
Or ought to.
Or should be.
I thought I understood this season.

September doesn't stand still for anyone—she is
walking past you   *look, you crumb*
of a leaf I shook down   *beg for me.*
She is tired—wanting but won't give an inch
because look how around the horizon
she darkens   so early in the day now.

press me against your chest and lightning

give fever to   *heat anything*

    stuff to reaction   *evaporation*

it isn't enough—just physical.

burn me, *I think.*   *that's how we'll cheat time.*

/ / /

[YOU DON'T KNOW NOTHING ABOUT ME]

You don't know nothing about me.

spat.

blasted.

So much of me is bayonet.

Bayonet. You be the

bayonet I'll be the

bayonet I'll be the

you the bayonet I'll be

the be the wound I'll be

the bayonet you be the

wound I'll be the wound

I'll be the bayonet wound

you be the wound I'll be the

wound you the bayonet you be

the wound I'll be the wound

You don't know how to

nothing about me.

/ / /

/ / uhoh / /

[C R A N K]

DAT CANKZZ, GIRL?
GOT U CANTANKEROUZ ! ?

CRANK SED

MAI BODEH 2
BOOOOTY LISHUZZ

BROODY WIT A BOOTY

DON'T LUK SEAUX
SAAAD, HUNNIE!

AY GIRRRRRRRRRRLLLLLL

WAT U GOT 2
B SAD ABT??

lol.

HA

nothin'   nothin'

nvm.

[be gracious, air]

When I sleep, I'm headed toward you
all the seconds become fake
or nothing.
I crave.

Bigmouth gasp, air —
take as much of you in
but even you this dark has become
inundated & wretch.

// [what beasts]

clawed their way

through the attic ceilings

    Open the door.

while I laid awake wondering —

how do you dig your way

to the sky? //

It's the inside that knows so much
nothing &

nothing

& nothing & I repeat
myself so far ahead of me
when I catch up, it echoes.

Thunder.

Memory resistant like a virus.

[SWELL]

The longing sinks in through newsland vomit. Teleportation sickness. I'm frozen. Stunned the people here are alive, not always so far away asleep inside their houses. Microwave dinner convenience. All the babies growing warm by the minute. All the tired dogs.

I stare out your window and pretend I have a garden. I plant flowers in the shape I think my name would take if names had shapes not made of letters. I make a cup with my hands to pat the soil down. I make a little wilderness humping up to this city.

I grow warm in your sheets by the minute. I'm a newborn, breath wet and sweet. At night I dream I am some dark eagle, and when I ride myself up into the sunset, I keep riding into the hazy after-sunset, past the past-the-horizon where it failed. I'm not at the edge of any season — not at the edge of anything, just here penniless and ugly and naked in bed — these human maneuvers. I'm still learning them all.

I wake and the people are toward something—active and I'm at the periphery. The innocence is so moving I want to cry. What I can't have. I'd kill for it. I'm sorry, I tell you. Sorry I woke up braised in brainfever, not belonging here. It's just that this place is fucking hungry. Hungry like a baby. Dream me somewhere else. I think you are creamy like a stuffed fuckin pastry. Come in, I'm a lighthouse. Come in. Come in. Underneath us, suburbia swells.

// Forest fires don't last too long here.
Too-wet ground, you know this.
In fact — did I mention? The prescribed
burn of longleaf pines along the 1–10
Corridor — painstaking — to scorch
nutrient vegetation, to preserve the
habitats of small, endangered animals.

Yesterday, I thought I saw
a lark
or sparrow —
a smear of sky //

// [something is coming for us.]

*— I don't know what it'll bring —
could you be so kind ....?*

*— Each is a needed thing, don't
you see? It needs to happen.
It's supposed to. Just pray.
God brought it to us. Just
pray.*

*— If you take it out of this place —
it dies —
may as well be dead.*

— A beast is still a beast even when it's dead. //

// [impression of a colored-something
summer]

                              what rain
        happened

                  and heat

your terrible
crotchlike heat. I'm incredibly
uncomfortable now   *now now*
Can you not? Can you hide it
somewhere better?

        Can

you

        inch lower? //

                              // come to the ground

                              I can find it. Heavy should

                              remorse be given

                              properly a burial

                              Musty weight summer —

                              gone — the dread

                              the season's change —

                              it sweat you out. //

35

// I'm gonna let it shine //

///

[bridge to me again]

my roof so strong my
house's insides still new —
the mortgage refinanced.

// BRRRRRIIIINNNNGGGG!!!!

BRRRIIINGGG!!!!!

look — the young flimsy
pines break their backs
to the wind as I sleep under
soft mountains of pillows —
BRRRRROOOOOOOOOMMMMMGGGGZZZZ!
or pillowed by
forgetfulness or hopeful
to wake in a better
NEWZ   UPCHUKD!
situation of stronger trees.
CHUNKD UP

but houses like paper sculptures — houses
so delicate when the wind rips high —
WAT THEY DO FOR A
almost nothing to them.

///

HOT LUNCH!

HOT LUNCH!

HOT HOT LUNCH!

upchuck

I holy
shit myself
I heard the news //

36

///

[CRANK SED]

Y'ALL   AIN'T   NEVER TASTED NAAH

SHIT   LIK   MINEZZZ

///

///

[unleashed]

what could be a beast to me

beast is a beast

even when it's dead

a human is a body

beast stays a beast even when

a man or a person or a body

a dead beast is still a beast

at best:
"so sorry, thank you."
"so sorry,
thank you," even when —

///

///

[I'M SO HAPPY B/C THINGS ARE VRY BEAUTIFUL]

That night the thing I can remember
a name like Christmas —
the too far-off season and never white
not here — never snows here —
Garland Robinette seems
the only voice left alive and Garland
Robinette — *like garlands like sparkles*
and robins in nests like baskets, like presents —
on the radio — It wasn't too bad, except
why is the water rising
if the storm is gone —

// [she lets me open my
windows to heavy sound]

I dream of a kiss

like a rainbridge

watermouth,

a stretch of a bridge

I'm sure in other places
the night doesn't darken
just empties its shadow—
figures lucid and temporary.

of water

vapor from

my mouth to yours

It is we are temporarily
fed on air and misfortune —
is that how we accumulate?

like strata — could we not —

I can't find my heels
at the floor of you.

What followed was a bend
in the trees when the wind had fired —

me, oblivious in my bed.

///

// Less the fog in the streets
more the moisture in the ground
lifted.

I think this dark is
the same dark you open
your eyes to see nothing at all.

It's not all unkind,
only just quiet
and a sense of space. //

Throat. Cage.

                    water can make a smear
                    appear more
                    broke

                    my meat hands
                    your throat —
                    my small hands.

                    ain't no one wanna throat me!

this week is diamonz

                    BUST.

            AWWWWWWWHHHHH SHIT.

///

[easy there, bird. easy.]

— mind the sense that says
if you venture too far
from the water
you will die

         — too sore to be the fringe of
         — too empty to be a mother to

something is coming for us

    each bad thing is a needed thing —
    don't you see?

                         just pray

if you take the bird out of its place

it dies — it may as well be dead.

               ///

///

emergency

don't know what home
sound like, smell like

they so obviously happy
so dead in the process don't
know how much we have left

tttthhhhuuuuuuuddupph......thhhhhhhhhuduphhh

what is the sound

of alarm

expected rhythm meaning

blasted

fell to the
ground, heavy

heaving, too
too migrant

refugee. itinerant
just pass through —

I CAN BLOW YOUR SHIT OUT THE WATER
TAKE THE AIR SWELL IT LIKE IT DON'T DRINK
THERE, BOIL ADVISORY
BRING IT TO MY DISTRICT — BET YOU CAN'T
BRING IT THERE

a body with a heart there
too, slammed down

appealing to

call the government!

nothing *thud*

thud

nothing

let the wind take me

ain't nobody's business but my own…

/ / /

///

[ALL THAT IS LEFT IN THE GAS CAN —]

Dad bought a new

truck that could swim
— said "I never want to feel
trapped again" I didn't
know if he was ever scared.

Power outage Thursday after
is tuna noodle casserole
cooked in the gas grill on the back
porch is hot in the house as it is
outside I wonder who will pick up the trees —
can they be grafted to themselves
back upright?

our little forest
how it littered with itself
splintered to the eyewall

what a waster of trees, then
what a master, that wind.

///

CHUNK.

// your undulating mouth //

//

ain't nobody got …

//

// what wound?

what a tender

tender tender like

food easily digested

tender tender like

given

tender like   *chewed. //*

//

…time…

//

45

///

I do remember the bridge.
It had me in its sights
in the fog that lingered.

I kept its voice close
— closer than the summer trees
closer than the river even
could bend.

///

///

[A CRUMB IN THE COBBLESTONE — TELL ME

THIS LANDSCAPE DARKENED WITHOUT YOU]

Say despite all the churches with their unlocked doors
and outstretched strangers' palmskin, *I hungered still.*

— squandered when, fell through like a crumb, I sat waiting
for discovery or disintegration *—something marvelous*
teething at the surface —a crumb, devotional, religious ecstatic

      closer to being *worthy*

Desire me ruthless and naked but still in my Sunday dress
you opened the window — we humid and slept open
into dreaming, *yes, conduit*. Conduit or nothing. Conduit
or bust. Nothing or busted. Hug the breakwater's edge

more the grit, my fingers — *whorl*, the inches of all
concrete make miles of this low, walled city.

Pretend expansive with me like *ocean.*

River. Lake. Bodies.

          if I said I was vessel — a container, not for sailing

          if I said I was vesselgirl, not leakyfaucetgirl
          so — drip

          it's not the same as carrying

                                ///

///

[I WOULDN'T TROUBLE YOU TO FIGURE THIS WEATHER OUT]

I had imagined something much
cleaner and neater lines I dream
plenty of bears and they chase me.

Swear I've been lucid every day, but this —
I went with the wind

[DNR —]

hopeful, baby

circumference
       moisture   *it's hopeful*
conclusion this:
empty-head   *opeful.*

unfurl. it takes energy to —
the sun uses itself up
      ope.

to autumn — my bright song
the clouds look sweet — tameable

      ope.

      ope.

you are one adorable baby

///

48

// [SWAG]

GURL—U SWAG

CRANK SED

SWAGGERIFFFFFFFFFFFFFFFIC!

I'LL CRUMB U
I'LL GASH U   *// do I conduit?*
GASHING GASH   some days I wish
I'LL UPCHUX U   conduit

                         was conduit

                         autopilot me off
CRANK SED   get a grip

                                   ow! oww!

                         this place got ugly //

DAT BROOZE WUZ
E D U C A T I O N A L //

/ / /

Now I live far from home in a small town where
the blinds are pulled down — shut, except for
mine. I realized walking up to my apartment
one evening, if someone in the street thought
to look up there they could see my big round
nipples, all puffy and private — my weird body
floating in the window, in its place, not seeking
revenge, not wanting those eyeballs — just pure
big nipple outward living.

/ / /

/ / /

[LUSSSSSHHHHH]

/ / /

LUSH is duh smellz
smellz in duh
gutter   fuk
o — fuk   o gutter

pardon. quiet quiet quiet if
I shut my eyes there will be
a feast set before me I can
GOBBLE IT ALL UP! ALL FOR ME
I can make it all mine all of it

a flower rupture
blossom chasm
wild wild
divide a tiny
canyon breaking

CLOSE IT DOWN!

the district is hurting again
mama says, cuz it can't find its shoes
to walk to higher ground
where rich people live

/ / /

I can't find my shoes either
I can't party in places I've *never* been
even though I want to

/ / /

/ /   hush   your   mouth   up   / /

50

// [go back to where you came from]

that place home?

is that place?—
can it be repeated through
my spine so I can travel there,
my feetself can take me
if it knows where to go

(depression location)
(desperation location) //

///

[Later, the pavement upset with waterweight]

never a drought for long —
the space a levee takes up

levee — a road of water to the lake,
the spillway, the brackish marsh
where I, like a damselfly, will hunt
for a sprig of grass to land

(we're losing it)

I'm hunting down water from the Marigny
to here. From the Canal St. Ferry
to the West Bank, where I saw you last
before they closed the bridge down.

///

// [Come all up this fever]

I cannot *can't* I hold so much

this table an anchor

this table a raft

all the faces don't even know me

// sleeps makes a delicate shape

on your wall the shadows there

tell us our bodies, wrapped inside,

this light / absence

why can't I become a builder myself?

sleeps cavorted with lola! said

— Panic cannot be everything.

— Sway it down.

she's good she's good

she rides all night

— Talk about it

— Oh, sure

a novel bruise!

what a novel bruise

you have there. //

What have you done?
What have you done? //

[Un]

The space is muttering to me. *Hinge. Pin. Anchor.*
Something to flex. Hazardous muscle. What I don't have.

Far away, I am breathing the driest air of my life. My insides —
a humid creature. I was born into it. When I was a month old
a volcano exploded, and mama said the ash was so thick it coated
my diapers black on the clothesline. I am something of my history —
creaturely. I try my mouth with sound but walls just echo it back to me.
If I opened a window to let the air out or in, would I fade outside into
the winter and seep most dangerously out of this small brown body —

You are sleeping far away, I know it when I sleep I'm headed toward
you — all the seconds become fake or nothing. I crave. Hungry again.
Hungry women put fingers into their mouths and suck it fills a hole it
feels like feeding. Inside knows so much of nothing and nothing and I
repeat myself so far ahead of me, when I catch up, it echoes. I had a
dream — memory, resistant like a virus. I am a blank one.

When I see you with all the lights crossed out, I want to sing. Into my
skin all day and let bounce off the wallpaper, let be loud enough to peel
it with my hands, allow it to shiver. To have enough, in my hands —
I break from the self —

/ / /

/ / River, your undulating mouth / /

/ / /

[YOU WERE BORN IN IDEAL CIRCUMSTANCES]

hanging by a pain

pillowmouthed

— under an oak tree

— in the cold
hospital chamber
outside of which my father
paced, too afraid
of blood or bad
luck to view
my crowning
infant head.

my mother cried for the flowers — already ordered
readied to precious the church

/ / /

// — Today
— Yesterday
— Ad nauseum

My mausoleum digitized

Always so terrible I
make the choice —
The sweet smell of cotton
candy and feces. Home
sweet home. / /

/ / /

[Scented with the death of you]

I tried to clean the air.

[Morbid procedure —] the river
had 1000 fingers to count off on

all of those wistful —
those lingering saids

I was fed up.
I was fed up on it.

coooooooooooooooooooooooool spill

dat cool spill

*Nostalgialicioussss! Nostradamushhy, 'cuz
I was a 14-year-old prophet living uphill
or as high as the ground could muster*

I tried to clean the air inside with the air outside
and I still — such still air — could not breathe

/ / /

/ / ....shine / /

// COTTON CANDY

SWEET TO GO

LET ME SEE THAT

TOOTSIE ROLL

COTTON CANDY

SWEET AS GOLD

LEMME SEE THAT

CANDY BOWL

COTTON CANDY

TOOTSIE ROLL

GONNA EAT YOUR

CANDY HOLE

COTTON CANDY

BOUGIE HOLE

I'MMA GETCHA CUNT

U HOE //

// my flight left home without me.

I combed Craigslist Missed Connections
but no one described what I was wearing,
the color of my hair — //

// [she wrote your name in vomit]

what happened *happened* — trivial
or mistaken. she took her feet to be prophetic —
her thirdeye toe to go with the wind

— feed everything to the birds
— be jointed, mellifluous again //

// Central is not a place you want to go to.

Central is a place I've never been.

— David says Central is a
   "way of life" and
— David says "white flight"
   and I say
— "in what sense?"
— David says "you really
   don't want to see for
   yourself—but they got a
   Dairy Queen" //

///

[Give me a home I can have]

Heat hangs its head low

I can bridge my
rhythm ebb
— flown
fog on my window
glass heat to make
sense of it

I pastel like a baby —
jump at the chance to feed
myself to the interstate.
To feel historical.

This is Whiskey Bay where he
dumped the bike before he dumped
her body — *a girl like me,*
my own age — I make habit myself
follow the speed limit

Living is not the way
bluer or grayer or
brown than the water
here *is my appendix showing*?

Vestigial, is my life located?
I merge with the pothole
and we become one.

How to explain to you
the Causeway is just a very long
bridge, 26 miles of
concrete continuous
water — span and I, the length of it
— the incredible lack of trees

And just horizon. Not even
big like the ocean or poem
the Gulf of me subsiding always
upsetting the shore used to
flow and flow never just stay put.

See how I stretch from north
to south — here?

You'll never dissolve

all this sand.

///

///

flatten them
fatten 'em
flatinum

FUCK! my name in DIAMONZ
blitz em with DIAMONZ
set it in PHATINUM

I'm gonna let it shine

///

// [Outcome]

doubtful, so
I'll marry myself a bridge.

I'll build a tiny house
tall if not straight
to accommodate the flood

if all else fails

we were too next door
to hear the neighbors drowning //

// i said to him
please carry the baby while
i iron these sheets

can't have said while
i'm working doubles
at the Dairy Queen

i just—don't know what to
do about it //

flooded the earthworms out
of the soil but the sun too hot
for them to make it across the driveway

// LAWD or LORD — LORDY
or LOUD

WHAT NAME DO I DO ABOUT IT? //

what
Is there a word for the simultaneous mistrust and fascination of ~~white~~ people?

//river, your kindly

undulating

mouth //

// safe space to drown

carotid, arterial

song song

song song song //

// meat components.

extra mild
or spicy.

crispy.
golden

crunch.

basic, with
biscuits. tender. fluffy. //

// [CRANK SED]

OOOOOOOOOOOOOOOOO!

DAT
BOOTIE

                    SHIT.

GIRL.

                              // i sprung so
                              fast to bruising
                              fat black itch

YOU IN IT. //   glitch in my construct
                              — take me there unhinge
                              coil — clean surface to
                              limn — time set
                              tick — tick hush tick
                              bone set bone clean
                              eat eat eat

                              bruise was educational //

/ / /

[Late summer, what I buried]

We evacuated to Florida — Mom and Dad and me, and Mom only after taking the long way home from Kenner Regional Hospital up through the Manchac swamp along I-55 because all the other bridges through the lake weren't just closed, they were broken. The storm surge had pulled the Twin Span off their piers and the police would catch you and make you turn around if you tried to cross the Causeway because *only emergency vehicles only* — no one should be on the roads, and if you weren't smart enough to leave before the storm, tough luck. But we couldn't leave Mom behind.

I don't remember Florida. Mom and Dad didn't make me go to school there — I don't know why — and I spent most of September asleep. I think. I had a cell phone. I didn't make many calls, I think. One night we had sushi, I think. I really don't remember much at all — not really anything. I only remember that when we got back home in October, the lights were working and the fridge didn't smell that bad and I went back to school and took the geography test I'd studied so hard for during the storm.

/ / /

*// I spent up all my miracles for two gallons of gasoline
and my own stretch of highway*

drove all the way up to Mississippi

If I fevered, would that push my sins to breaking? //

///

absence. 'scape.

wet and frightening is
the trees sting with you

what was mine all
heavy than before

saltmines. salt water.
metals coil and trash.

the egrets beat their wings off
for desperation. for the heavier

you. dismantle the bloat
the tired ghosts, all your reminders
unburied, bloat the water.

///

*// AAAYY, GIRL!
HEY, DON'T LET IT GET U*

DOWN //

///

[Keep it clean]

Lake is big and the light on the water makes a shimmery dress on it—
Give me a day all sunsets with the wide colors riding up its back,
flooding the sky. Wander these streets when the sun gets high so
hot wonder — *if I were made of more moisture, how quickly could I
evaporate?* — stand still and the sky is heat lamps, and I'm willing the
soles of my shoes to melt me to the blacktop. *I could watch from here.*
The road is the halflight makes the cracks and the edges and shadows
make them deeper. *How is something animated in stillness?*

Ten miles away from the city is water. And after? The horizon. The
skin feels like it's burning without shelter.

///

// [SPIT]

AAWWHH SHIT

I MIX SO BRITELY WITH IT

I JUZ BLAZE WITH IT —

BUMP IT — BIG OL' EASE

*YEAH, UR GUUD, UR
GUUD — U RIDE ALL NITE //*

///

Never gentle —
only so light

CRANK SED I was
brilliantly morbid

give me a
great big
mouth i can
shadow in the
distance is half
ominous and swollen —
it makes me wet
when it rains; dad
says i'll get struck by
lightning
but it's the thunder

i say —
i have a perfectly red heart.

i adapt to the bus schedule.
i let some black men stare @me &
wonder if my skin
tastes like salt caramel i let some
white men stare @me &
wonder what color my mama is
if i'm adopted if i
speak in inglish
if i'm 12 yrs old

[CRANK SED]　　if i'm good in bed

i'd rather play with
thunder, far
off from the coast,
moving in —
sound so big to
blow me away

sound so big it moves me

ROSEBUD, AW HELL
SO PRETTY & SO
DAMN SAD

YOU'RE AS PURE AS
AN ACETYLENE BABY
GIRL

i stare at how my thighs have ballooned to
cellulite. when they say "oppressive"
it means it's so hot you don't want to go
outside you don't want to move.

how it tears at me & don't want it to end

you are so pure

YIELD UR POLITIX
UP TO MEME

— SEZ they are "wear shoes inside the
　　house" kind of people
— SEZ maybe I can be an egret
— SEZ its ok to sleep all days long
— SEZ our timeline gone bad

COLLECT
TO MAKE URSELF
HAPPY

legit ghosts give me
chills when i get nervous
when i must speak and
i'm so sexy that i don't
know how.

my mother is the color of a diamond

///

67

[ROAD HOME]

nothing.

nothing for weeks

bleak.

looks bleak.

then months.

fucking bleak.

//[Loot]

....doesn't care about

black people   (can't talk about it)

race card   (can't say that word)

Even me — I would be a hypocrite
because I had to turn away from the TV
because it was too hard to watch.

taboo body

elicit body

// [KYOOT LI'L MONSTA TEETH]

— *GONNA FEEL GUUD ON UR COCK*
U GONNA FALL ON YA COCCYX
YA ASSBONE //

// Zack says: *I walk home drunk a lot. There's never anyone out that early except old black men who go fishing in the lake and old white men who go power-walking. //*

// CAN'T
NEVAH
                                                        // who dat
                                                        say dey gon'

GIT WUT
                                                        eat
                                                        my
U DON'T EARN   whole?

&

U CAN'T

HOLD   // things that closed
                stayed closed but still   who dat?
WUT U JUST   take up space

SHUT DOWN   —is it there if we're   who dat?
                not allowed inside?

                silent things can't always hide themselves

DON'T
                I get nauseous trying to find —   say dey gon
NEVER HOLD

WUT U JUST

SHIT OUT
                                                        eat me hole //

& THEN IT'S
GONE //

70

shut me
out something
fearful I'm scared of
rabies and heatstroke

horrible all the water //

/ / /

[Tired Ghosts]

luck   (does this look

infected?)

— *baby*
baby
                    you, my aftermath —

I'm gonna
cradle you till

                                    luck —

            a forethought

        my   then troubled by
    stink   translation
            flow

            red   you
                        decay / fracture

                    between disintegration and completion

does this   body, colored—*thump*

        make a sound?

                                / / /

// I am my mother's

very sad

only little ghost //

Now I live in a town where the twilight is lucid — it
doesn't break me — it's not beauty enough to. But there
is an almost-starlight and a jet engine jumbo jet making
lines into the sky — wish I were so straight and narrow.
So fast and thin.

The cicadas are out again this year, like that hot
autumn you called them "*kings*." Where are you now?
Something like the wind blew you away — just like you'd
threatened—

But do you envy me? — here in my cold room that
is mine because I pay for it. What do you lust for?
(If you've found lust…) Do you crave a more natural
honey? Do you crave a cheaper, sweeter apple?

Here the windows are like mirrors and the mirrors like—

Do you mind?

Did you ever?

As in—do you know what it means? — what I paid for?

// mother mattered
don't forgette her
ere the tide
rides hung
hug the wind

the wind — forgetter //

Nobody   got   time

     left us   wandering   because the *lostness*   was

                                        not yet

          impermeable

Nobody got time because the lostness got time

// [Y'all got dat]

cool spill

dat cool spill

dat cooooooooo oooooooooo oooooooooooooooooooooool

spill //

// I dreamt again my teeth
were falling out
and as my gums receded,
I recounted all the things
I'd done wrong //

[BINGE]

It's dark up to my knees,
the binge limit
the streets get sour after
ten o'clock it's hard to walk
during this time of night.

Hesitation is lacking
and I'm free here—not as wide
but there's comfort
there, the black road—broken
down to the insides where moisture seeps in
— the way the street narrows to meet you
then melts away

///

// SED

— GIRRRRRRL

DO U KNO?

WHEN U WHIP UR
ASS ROUND
LIKE A FREAKDAMN
SHOWPONY—

WUT U
THINK GONNA
HAPPEN?

WUT U
THINK
GONNNA HAPPEN

2 UR SWEET
CARAMEL ASS? //

///

I'd always felt the temporary
girl, swollen like I held in me
too much water or salt.

Ask more when I say — make
me free — that beautiful color
maximized by the weight of its opposite.

How it stabilizes the little ground I live on.

Make a memory on it

Make a little

licky ˙

strain

edges — but even further

— if I hassle it, will it go?

///

78

// [MORE SURFACE]

let me
fondly

dig my way to a map //

[TWISTED UP. A MAGNOLIA BUD]

what word for
the arch of a foot needing balance?

finger to wriggle the teeth
in an open mouth *pluckpluck*
— like that easy.

glass me a body
a fortuneteller mouth

sees the world inside a porcupine fruit
a stop on the streetcar line
where a dame-like mute sits
with eyes absorbed in daylight

how glassy her eyes like the lake
is glassy before the spillway *— it opened*
— how it hurts my heart
to be away
I think about Jesus
when I am away when

I hear Jesus

when

I hear bells

draw lines as a kind of forgetting —
what does it drive a body to?

when I led myself and you
out onto the breakwater —
something was lost

///

Lover, the day we drove down to the Abbey
and stalked the gravestones, Mother Mary statuesque
— her concrete arms outstretched — yes, the
longing —
I had it, and she —

I wanted to see the longing in her.

Remember when I googled "vespers" — a word I'd
familiarized but confused with "vigil," like the twilight
and dawn were just positions — the sun againing itself,
but different somehow. To reset. Or to replay. To
comfort me.

///

[For the periphery, burning]

what is good enough for the thick skin to ride it?

One: Always to map out the direction of memory
peeling — in-growing upon itself

Two: Harden in the light —
fresh clayed humans are deeply ebbed and flown —

Three: From this place, the eeriness pervasive —
the skin half-severed
within an inch of its life

look how it holds on —

///

*// Mass has several meanings
one of which is to
fingers down your throat or
relive your education //*

// [Tired Ghosts]

This is imperative.

This is you do
rightly by it.

O Angel.

*edge. garden. song
peripheral burning.*

The chemicals what stained
my dress

embrace me
no one cares enough to
meet me

What is shelter?

— told me once
it is knowing how
to open into open
how many words are
there for —opened?

blasted.

reluctance survived me

water's what stained my dress

bruise was educational

I'd drown in this shallow lake
if I didn't know how to swim
all the trees dead on the bottom / /

WIND (crank) // WIND (air)
WOUND (hole) // WOUND (cranked)

// hide me

inside

we

inside //

[sic] we tried
[sic] we tired
[sic] we tread
[sic] we tire
[sic] we tided
[sic] we tide red
[sic] we tied red
[sic] we tried read
[sic] we tired ride
[sic] we tired
[sic] we tried
[sic] we tried

[TENDER]

tender is my
foot in the door
foot in the mouth tongue
in the cheek of the roof
of the mouth, tender chunk
so infant I fire
without it expelled
a violence

the heat hangs it head low.
it doesn't velvet out of me
to say so.

say —

NEEDED: recipient
ADDRESS: sad

SED:
body needs location or
without space, it empties.
it bodies quickly gap-quiet
block. cell. make up. body
space or
liquid to fill it

or — air on top
air — hydrated
air — filled
air — a capacity
possibly — lungs, a smell
when alive —
atrophy when
post-post mort

after death,
fill the container left

un

sed — CRANK

SED

UM...

river made me shit myself rotten

I'm gonna go down to the ground where it fed me

I've waited too long under the loam

uhoh   come a-knockin'

come a-knockin'

a-knockin'

PAGE 6: "ain't nobody got time" initially references Kimberly "Sweet Brown" Wilkins' viral video with the heavily memed "ain't nobody got time for that" expression. PAGE 8: [Tips & Tricks] was adapted from a popular email chain post titled "Safety Tips for Women Written by a Cop" or "Though a Rapist's Eyes (PLS TAKE TIME TO READ THIS. It may save a life.)" from the "If I knew what is 'Love' It's Bcoz of 'You'..." Facebook page. PAGE 10: "You're either local or you're not" is taken from the slogan of Rouses Supermarkets, a popular regional chain of Louisiana-based grocery markets. PAGE 14: The checklist is adapted from a FEMA hurricane preparedness brochure. PAGE 21: "THANK YOU THANK YOU THANK YOU JESUS JESUS JESUS" is taken from a live Kermit Ruffins performance at the Blue Nile jazz club. PAGE 32: Garland Robinette's coverage on WWL 870 AM radio station was the only live broadcast to continue in the New Orleans area during Hurricane Katrina and its aftermath. PAGE 37: "ain't nobody's business but my own..." uses Taj Mahal, "Nobody's Business But My Own" PAGE 49: "cotton candy and feces. Home sweet home" Thank you, Aubrey Allison PAGE 50: "COTTON CANDY SWEET TO GO..." uses several misheard lyrics from The 69 Boyz, "Tootsee Roll." PAGE 51: "Central" is Central City, Louisiana in East Baton Rouge Parish, not the Central City neighborhood of New Orleans. PAGE 60: "You're as pure as an acetylene baby girl" Thank you, Justin Wymer. PAGE 61: "Even me ..." fragment is a quotation taken from Kanye West's comments during a Hurricane Katrina relief benefit telethon on NBC. PAGE 62: "who dat say dey gon..." is adapted from the popular New Orleans Saints chants and songs.

// [ACKNOWLEDGMENTS]

Excerpts of this book have appeared in these publications, some in different forms: [Maggot-breathed, she was so sweet it all] first appeared in *The Bat City Review*; [This story survived up stream of me] and other excerpts appear in *agápē*; gratitude to the editors.

Thank you to the Iowa Writers' Workshop, especially Connie Brothers, Jim Galvin, Jan, and Deb. Thank you to Iowa friends and colleagues for your brilliance and spirit, for the time and kindness you've given to this book at various stages. To my teachers, especially Laura Mullen, Joyelle McSweeney, and D.A. Powell—so much magic. Tremendous gratitude to everyone at Futurepoem, especially Dan Machlin, Carly Dashiell, and JT. Thank you to Tom and Jessica of Everything Studio.

Deepest thanks forever to those writers, readers, and friends who have given this book and me their care, attention, and support. To Dini Parayitam—you invaluable life and friend; Zachery Elbourne, Justin Wymer, Fatima Espiritu, Alice Gribbin, David Kruger, Avro Chakraborty, Jessie Hennen, and David Benedetto.

To my parents, Jesse Marchan and Victoria D. Marchan—love and gratitude in oceans.

// [Jerika Marchan] was born in Manila, Philippines. She lives in New Orleans. This is her first book. //

nonchalantly as he got on his bike.

"Oh, yea," I nodded, trying not to laugh.

"Thank your girlfriend and your little buddy for help-ing me last night." He began to peddle away.

"And thank you, Larry, for pulling ..." I couldn't finish. He turned the corner and disappeared like a flying sau-cer.

I called and asked my friend Gina to use her com-puter to try to find anything on Nicholas Pushkin. Gina had helped me before on cases and was always able to find something important. Not this time. She came up empty. I sat around my house that night stuck on the case and it didn't get any better Sunday morning. I read the paper but there was nothing worth noting except Ev Capshaw's first real byline titled "Police Deny Frantic 91 Call." It was a rehash of what I had witnessed in the con-ference room, and also how an unidentified source pro-vided her a recording of the call. There was also a sill picture on page three of Joe and me sledding down th hill. My investigation had hit a roadblock, so I spent th rest of Sunday studying for my make-up test for Mr. Re sons and praying for more snow. There was talk of a other 'big one,' but reality slapped me in the face Mond morning when my clock radio went off and the said, "...a great song by The Samples. Now for the weather. V are going to get hit again but it won't start till arou noon. So get up sleepyheads or you'll miss that big yell school bus!"

"One question, though. Why did you change your mind?"

"I might not tell you. But, someday I will let you know. And remember I vas smiling when I told you this."

Hilda was speaking in riddles, but I smiled and said, "I'll remember, Hilda. I'll remember."

Even though I had no clue what the cover-up was all about, I felt sure of two things—it had to deal with the CIA and Nicholas Pushkin. How were they connected? Two theories bounced around in my head as I trudged past Bill's Donuts. Either Pushkin was an agent for the CIA and they had him declared dead so he could take on a new identity and continue working for them, or they were after him for playing a part in the broad-shouldered man's death. Maybe the broad-shouldered man was a CIA agent, and that's why they were after him? That would be an-other reason why the CIA had the Belltown Police de-clare Pushkin dead. Pushkin might think he got away with it and come out of hiding—that is, if he wasn't hiding in the bottom of the ocean, waiting for a fish net to find him. I shuddered at the thought as I glanced over at the dumpster behind Bill's Donuts. I spotted Larry, the home-less man, putting soda cans in a bag. I wanted to ask him why he took off after we helped him at the carnival. I thought it had been kind of rude.

"Hey, Larry. What's up?"

Larry answered, "Nuthin'."

"Larry, I was wondering why you left us hanging with Officer Coughlin last night at the carnival?"

He looked up from his bag. "Sorry, I didn't want to get in trouble 'cause I didn't pay to get in."

"Oh, OK. I understand. See ya." All I wanted was an explanation so I began to walk away when he said, "Can you believe this?" His filthy hands held up a plastic soda ring made to hold six-packs.

"What about it?"

"These things are made for seagull hunting." Larry ripped the rings apart.

"Seagull hunting? No one hunts gulls on the Cape."

"Not on purpose. But people put these soda rings in the trash and they don't realize that if a gull picks through the garbage it could get its head caught in one of the rings, and snap!" he snapped his fingers, "broken neck. Dead gull. I hate to see dead gulls. 'Cause sea gulls are the Cape's angels looking down at us."

"I agree." And I did. I always thought there was something special about the gulls.

"Did you find your flashlight?" Larry asked as he went back to his work.

"Flashlight?"

"Yeah, I threw it by the dunes . . ." Larry poured out some soda from a near empty-can and flung it into his bag.

"Wait, Larry, you're the guy who pulled me out of the ocean this morning?"

"Yup."

"Why did you take off?"

"Sometimes I put my tent up on Breakers B cops have caught me a lot. They said the next t catch me they're going to have me committed. So take off. Don't tell no one."

"Committed for just sleeping on the beach?"

"Well, they also think I'm nuts," he laughed, "but have to tell you about my nickname—Looney Lar made a crazy face.

"Only a few stupid people call you that." I tri brush over the subject. I have to admit though, somet Larry was out there and sometimes he was sharp as a Many people didn't know what he suffered from. So said he was a former boxer who was punch-drunk, oth thought he was a war vet who was shell-shocked. On t day, he seemed to know what was going on, so I decid to ask him a couple of questions.

"When I walked out on the jetties, I saw fresh foo prints. Did you see who made them?"

"That was me." He tied up his bag and then secured it to the back of his bike. I wondered how he was going to be able to ride his beat-up ten-speed on the poorly plowed streets.

"What were you doing on the jetties in the middle of the night?"

"I go out there sometimes to look at the UFOs." He didn't blink. He was serious.

"UFOs?" I raised my eyebrow.

"Yeah, unidentified flying objects. Now and then one appears for a couple of seconds in the middle of the night. But I haven't seen any in a few months," Larry said

"The party's over," I grumbled as I forced the covers off.

The snow started to fall earlier than the weatherman predicted and the words half-day were quickly spreading from student to student and teacher to teacher. Our principal, Mr. Finn, finally confirmed the whispers on the intercom at the beginning of fifth block, "All students and faculty will be dismissed after fifth block." A loud cheer echoed throughout the building. That meant I didn't have to stay after school to make up the test, I realized. I couldn't believe my luck. And for fifth block, all I had was study hall in the cafeteria, so that basically meant my school day was over. Mr. Cali, an English teacher and a study hall monitor must've sensed our excitement.

"Gang, this period you can talk to your friends as long as you don't get too loud."

We were all smiles as we put our books aside. My buddy Scotty Donovan raised a paper football in his hand and said to me, "You're all mine, Jacques!"

I smiled back, "Bring it on, Donovan."

My smile quickly faded as Mr. Reasons appeared holding a piece of paper in his hand. He whispered into Mr. Cali's ear, gave me a quick smile, turned and walked out of the cafeteria. I knew what was coming as I tapped the paper football with my pinky across the table hoping I was wrong.

"Orville, could you come here?" Mr. Cali waved his finger to me.

"It's my turn when you come back." Scotty made it clear.

"I won't be coming back," I muttered to myself and headed for the executioner.

"Mr. Reasons says you have to take this test and I'm supposed to monitor you. Sorry, buddy." Mr. Cali was genuinely sympathetic. After all, it was a math test and he was an English teacher. I tried giving it my best shot, but it was futile. After about twenty minutes, I gave up and just wrote down anything. For example, "The meaning of Z is it's the last letter in the alphabet." I had won a few battles with Reasons but he had won the war. I was going to flunk yet another Algebra test.

"Here you go, Mr. Cali." I tried handing it to him but his head was buried in the newspaper.

"This is terrible." He said to himself as he kept reading, "Oh, man. This is really horrible."

"What?"

"This obituary on Nicholas Pushkin, the man they found near Breakers Beach."

"Yeah, it's tragic." I agreed.

"Oh yeah, it's tragic how he died and all but that's not what I meant." He looked up from the paper at me.

"What do you mean?" I was puzzled.

"You were in my English class. Read the obit and tell me what I mean." He handed me the paper and I peered down and read:

In what can be described as a
Very tragic event for
All of the fishing community in Belltown
Nicholas "Radar" Pushkin, 64, was recovered from the
    sea.

In the two years Mr. Pushkin
Sailed and fished he became a friend to many.
He will be sorely missed by the fishing club.
Everyone who wants to donate in
Radar's memory can send their gift to
Environmental Friends of Cape Cod, P.O. Box 81,
    Belltown, Ma.

Maybe I'll check out the Environmental Friends of Cape Cod, I thought; they might be able to give me some info on Pushkin.

"So?" Mr. Cali waited for my response.

"So what?" I had no clue what he was talking about.

"Come on, Orville, your dad's an English teacher. He would drop dead if he knew you couldn't pick up the mistakes."

"I'm … it's sad and brief. Is it too short? I don't know."

"The beginning of each line is capitalized." He pointed down at the paper.

"Yeah, 'cause it's the beginning."

"Orville, just because it's the beginning of the line doesn't mean it's the beginning of the sentence."

"Oh man, you're right." I laughed. I couldn't believe it had slipped by me. But who really takes notice of punctuation errors when they're reading someone's obituary? No one probably, except for English teachers!

"Also, Orville, it says 'everyone who wants to donate in Radar's memory'. The proper English is 'anyone who wants to donate in Radar's memory.' I have a mind to call the Belltown News and let them in on their errors." Mr. Cali was disgusted.

"Yeah, you do that." I wanted to laugh at how passionate he was on the topic. I would have liked my Dad to see it. He had the same passion. But, he was in Ireland as an exchange teacher. "Mr. Cali, are you done with the paper?"

"It's all yours, Orville. I'm getting sick looking at it."

"Thanks. Oh and here's my test." I handed him the test and there were still another ten minutes before we could go home. I took out my notebook to copy down the Environmental Friends of Cape Cod's address. I glanced at the obit and then scribbled the P.O. box number 81, or was it 61? I checked again—81. This time the capital letters stuck out and I had to chuckle at the thought of how Mr. Cali was going to drop a dime to the editor. But then my mind said, Wait a minute, and I stopped my laughter and stared at the capital letters again. They were all set up under each other. I saw something. I took my pen and darkened the capitals to be positive.

In what can be described as a
Very tragic event for
All of the fishing community in Belltown
Nicholas "Radar" Pushkin, 64, was recovered from the
    sea.
In the two years Mr. Pushkin
Sailed and fished he became a friend to many.
He will sorely be missed by the fishing club.
Everyone who wants to donate in
Radar's memory can send their gift to
Environmental Friends of Cape Cod, P.O. Box 81,
    Belltown, Ma

My eyes were wide as I was fixed on the letters and what they spelled—**IVAN IS HERE**. The bell rang, shaking me out of my state. It could have been a coincidence but my gut told me that those capitals weren't typos or poor editing. They were there for a reason—to send a message. But to whom? And who was Ivan? I didn't have the answers, but I felt sure of one thing: the roadblock in my investigation had just been removed.

Chapter
Six

ON MY WAY to the *Belltown News* office, I spotted Larry riding his bike down Main Street.

"Larry," I shouted, and waved to stop him. He didn't hear me and was soon out of sight.

I had wanted to really thank him for saving my life. It was finally starting to sink in—I was extremely lucky that he had been on Breakers Beach in the dead of night.

"If not, then who knows ..." I whispered to myself.

"Who knows what?" Eve Capshaw's voice shook me out of thought.

"Oh, hi, Eve. Who knows when this snow is going to stop?" I said, thinking on my feet.

"The weather people sure don't know. There are whispers around town that the weather people better be working on their résumés." She laughed and I joined in.

"So, are you here for those negatives of Joe and you sledding?" Eve asked as I held the office door for her.

"Ah, no. I'm actually here for a project for my English class." I had worked out my cover on the walk over.

"Why don't you come over to my desk."

"You have your own desk? Wow, you are moving up the ladder," I smiled.

"Actually, it's Brian Jordan's. He's sick with the flu and that's why I was able to cover that story the other day."

"Oh yeah, that's right, that was a great story. How did you get that tape, anyway?"

I thought I'd give it a shot. Eve burst into laughter. "Like I'm going to spill my guts to you, Orville. Nice try."

"I was just curious."

"I've heard about your curiosity. Anyway, a reporter never reveals her sources."

"Wait. What do you mean 'your curiosity'?"

"I may be new to this town but I'm also a reporter. So are you really here for an English assignment, or are you playing kid detective?"

I wanted to gulp but I couldn't show any signs that she pinned it right on the head.

"Fair enough question considering my past. But Eve, I have to laugh because all I'm here for is to get some extra credit in Mr. Cali's class."

"Does this have to do with the obit on Nicholas Pushkin?"

"Well, yeah. How did you know that?"

"Mr. Cali called my editor, Mrs. O'Conner, about twenty minutes ago. He used to be her teacher so he gave her a friendly earful. Of course, Mrs. O'Conner passed it on to me because I wrote the Pushkin obit."

"So Mrs. O'Conner edited the obit and missed the typos." Or put them in, I thought.

"No. The writer always wants to blame the editor, but

I wrote and edited the obit. But I was only writing it the way the customer requested."

"Customer? What are you talking about?"

"Pushkin's friend, Perry Dowd," Eve said.

"Perry Dowd." I repeated.

"He's a scientist at the Belltown Oceanographic. You may have read about him in the paper."

"Oh, yeah." Dr. Dowd was always in the paper for some scientific event or another.

"He's a strange one, Orville. I mean, I pointed out the mistakes and he demanded I write it that way. He said it made it look poetic. Between you and me there is nothing poetic about it. But, who am I to tell him? That would have been kind of insensitive. Don't you agree?"

"You're absolutely correct." I tried not to smile but inside I was glowing. I was positive I was getting closer. But to what?

I went home and grabbed a bite to eat before I began my search for Dr. Dowd.

It wasn't hard to find out where Dr. Perry Dowd lived. My fingers did the walking through the Belltown phone book—Dowd, 32 Old Oyster Rd, Beltwn. The hard part was the other walking that had to be done. Old Oyster Road was about nine or ten miles away.

"There is no way I'm going to walk that far in this weather or any other weather for that matter," I grumbled to myself as I flipped to the Yellow Pages and looked for the word Taxi.

"There we go." I dialed the number and waited.

"Hello, you have reached the Belltown Village Taxi Service. We are sorry to inform you that due to poor driving conditions all taxi services in Belltown are closed."

"Closed, due to poor driving conditions? Isn't that the whole point of having taxis?" I said to myself, and hung up the phone.

I knew there was only one person who could help me out of this jam—Gina Goldman. Gina was my only friend who had a license, and she was the only person I knew who had a truck that could handle the poor weather. My dilemma was, did I want to involve her? Sure, I had involved her, in a way, by asking her to find out anything she could on Nicholas Pushkin. But, at the time, I told her it was because Mom thought Pushkin might be a distant relative. It was a white lie to keep Gina out of danger. After all, it was only the week before that I had put her life in jeopardy while working on another case. Gina came through that case with flying colors and was mad that I hadn't included her from the beginning. I knew if I included her now it wouldn't just be to drive. She would want to be in it for the whole nine yards, and whatever those nine yards included!

I also knew I had to tell her everything: Hilda's powers, Pushkin, the CIA. EVERYTHING. No more white lies because I wanted to give Gina a choice even though I knew what her answer would be. She was almost as bad as I when it came to wanting to find the truth. That is why it was a tough decision because it was really my decision, and I would have to live with the consequences. What am I going to do? I asked myself. I stared at the phone for five minutes before picking up and dialing.

"Hey, Gina. I need your help."

"I hate when you can't tell me stuff on the phone. This better be good, Orville. I had to tell my Mom that Karate class wasn't cancelled so I could get out of the house. I never lie to my Mom unless it's a good reason like …" Gina was trying to think of one while she brushed the snow off her coat.

"Like a case." I filled in the sentence.

"Are you serious?" She smiled.

"Dead serious." I said but there was no smile on my face.

I spent our driving time filling Gina in on everything. If we hadn't been through a couple of crazy cases before she probably would have been skeptical. I know I would have! But she believed everything, even Hilda's ability to touch an object and see the future.

We had been driving fifteen minutes at a pace of about twenty miles an hour.

"It probably would have been faster to walk," I said, while staring out the window at the snowy night sky.

"I can't go any faster or we might end up driving into a ditch or a pond or something." Gina's eyes were focused on the road.

"Well, as long as you don't drive into Pilgrim Pond," I laughed, referring to my last case, where that actually almost happened.

"Hey, if it wasn't for this truck your girlfriend might

not be your girlfriend. This truck saved her life and your social life," Gina giggled.

"She's not my girlfriend."

"Oh, did I hit a sore spot?"

"Whatever." Whatever always meant change the subject. Gina got the picture.

"Orville, are you positive you heard Officer Jameson say, 'I hate the CIA' and not 'I hate a DOA' as in Dead On Arrival? He may have been talking about the victim."

"Gina, I heard what I heard. He was talking about the guys who talked down to him—the CIA"

"The CIA, it just sounds kind of crazy. Don't you think?"

"And having a fortune-teller help isn't crazy! All of this is crazy, Gina, but that doesn't mean it's not true." I didn't like the idea that the one person who never questioned my hunches was doing just that.

"Hey, speaking of crazy, Gina, why aren't you playing any of your disco?" We all have our flaws and Gina Goldman's love for disco music ranked high on the list of hers.

"My radio busted the other day when I was listening to the Bee Gees."

"Thank God for small miracles. The radio probably couldn't take it any more." I laughed.

Gina cracked a smile but then said, "Look, Old Oyster Road." She pointed at the street sign.

Gina and I were like partners in a cop show. We had been killing time by joking around until we arrived at our destination, Old Oyster Road. That's when the laughter became silence. We were all business as the truck's headlights scanned the addresses on the mailboxes. After we rolled past a few houses Gina pointed, "Thirty-two. It's on my side."

"Kind of scary looking," I said, eyeing the old-style Victorian house, which was in complete darkness. There were three trash barrels lined up on the edge of the front yard, and the driveway was vacant.

"Orville, looks like he's not home. He must've gone away because his barrels are the only ones out in the whole neighborhood."

"Good point. I should have checked, though, to see if he has a wife or any children. Someone might be taking a nap or something." I rubbed my chin in thought.

"He's a bachelor in his early seventies. Lives alone," Gina said matter-of-factly.

"How do you know that?"

"The elderly women at the beauty parlor talk about him all the time."

"You're awesome, Gina. Now we can go ahead with plan A."

"Which is?"

"Pretty simple. We'll park up the street and then walk back here, and sneak into his house and search for clues." I pulled a flashlight and a hammer out of my duffel bag.

"We'll sneak in? Don't you mean *break* in?" Gina raised her eyebrows.

"Thieves break in. We are investigators. We sneak in. But, if you're not up for it, I . . ."

"No, I'm up for it. But Orville, if you're wrong about all of this we could really get busted." Gina jerked the truck into gear and headed up the road. She parked behind a snowdrift and then looked at me. "One question."

"Yeah, go ahead."

"If he had been home …" She stopped.

"Yeah?" I pushed.

"What was plan B?"

"Your guess is as good as mine, partner." I winked, trying to lessen the tension, opened the door, and hopped out.

"Well, I just hope you included bail money in your plan, partner." Gina shook her head before following me into the blizzard of the unknown …

Before we had the old Victorian house in our sights, I was excited and raring to go. In fact, I wasn't nervous at all about "breaking" into Dr. Dowd's house. Of course, my fearlessness turned and tumbled when we reached his backyard. My mind began to second-guess the idea. It was similar to the feeling of calling someone for a first date and then deciding to hang up out of fear of rejection. But before you can hang up, the person has already answered the phone, and there is no turning back. You have to face the fear head on. I wanted to hang up this idea but before I knew it, we were peering through the window of Dowd's back door. There was no turning back!

"Here. Hold the flashlight. Keep it low to the ground," I whispered, and Gina nodded. I raised the hammer and aimed for one of the windowpanes above the doorknob. The wind was howling furiously every couple of seconds so I waited. I figured I'd camouflage the sound of the smashing window by using the wind's thrashing. My arm was cocked and set when a loud bang made me jump and Gina turned the light automatically in the direction of the sound.

"What was that?" I whispered loudly.

"Look!" She pointed the light at the bulkhead that led to the cellar. The wind was tossing one of the bulkhead doors up and down like a rag doll. Gina ran over and I followed. She flashed the light onto the lock. It was unlocked.

"Orville, almost every bulkhead on the Cape is locked till spring. Why not this one?" she whispered.

"Maybe we're not the only ones here. Check for footprints."

Gina scanned the area but there were no visible prints other than our own.

"That's a relief. Dowd probably went on a trip and just needed something out of the cellar and forgot to lock the door," Gina said. I nodded in agreement, then shut the door, and headed back towards the rear door of the house.

"Pssss, Orville." Gina waved me back to the bulkhead.

"What?"

"Why break a window and risk being heard when we can get in the house through the cellar?" Gina didn't wait for my answer as she pulled the door open and pointed her light down into the pitch-black pit. Then she hesitated for a moment.

"Give me the light and I'll go first," I volunteered.

"I can handle it." The tone in her voice said, "Don't even argue." So, I didn't. We each cautiously made our way down the half-rotted wooden steps until we reached the dirt floor of the cellar. The winter-fresh air was replaced with a dank and musty smell. Gina slowly waved the flashlight around revealing old dusty cobwebs that contained a few living spiders, but mostly brittle remains. We pushed them away and continued on. The cellar was silent and felt tomblike except for a droning sound coming from the corner. Gina read my mind and threw the light at the sound—it was the oil burner. The light moved on finding nothing except more cobwebs and a couple of flying bugs. A strong sense of movement gripped me. I tugged on Gina's coat. "To the left." The shaking light just caught the tail end of a family of gray rodents scurrying into the cracks of the walls for safety.

We both twitched but kept moving forward.

I began to notice that the droning sound of the oil burner was beginning to be overtaken by another sound.

"What's that sound? I can't describe it," I said to Gina as we stopped to listen.

"I don't know. It's like a low hum. I don't like it." Gina was getting scared. I was, too, but I knew we didn't have much farther to go to the stairway.

"This cellar can't get much larger. I bet the stairway is around that corner." I tried to sound confident but the hum was getting louder and more synchronized, and I had this strange feeling of movement all around us.

"Since this house is pretty big that sound is probably another oil burner," Gina said.

"Could be." I hoped she was right.

We were about to turn the corner when I felt the movement again.

Someone was in front of us.

"Gina, to your right!"

Gina drew her light like a sword and stabbed the dark. "Nothing, Orville. Just a few flying bugs."

"Sorry." I wiped my sweaty brow.

"It's OK. I've had that same feeling like something is moving around us," Gina whispered again as we slowly edged around the corner.

"Gina, do you hear that sound?" I asked in a hushed voice.

"Yeah, it's getting more pronounced. Like ... like ... oh, wait. There are the stairs." We picked up the pace and were at the foot of the stairs when the sound became overwhelming.

"It's a loud buzz. Yeah, that's how I'd describe it," Gina turned back to tell me before moving the light slowly up each step until ... "AAAAAGH!" We both screamed at the lifeless eyes staring back down at us. I had never seen anything like it. There, sitting upright on the top step was the dead body of Dr. Dowd covered in a swarm of buzzing bees. Hundred and hundreds of buzzing bees ...

The sight made Gina drop the flashlight and it rolled across the floor until it finally rested, casting a thin beam on the cracked walls.

"Get the light!" we both yelled each not knowing where the other one was. I ran toward the light when suddenly the beam moved and pointed at me. She must've picked it up, I figured.

"Let's go!" I yelled, and the light moved closer.

"Well, stay in one place so I can come to the light!" Gina yelled back.

"Come to the light? I don't have the flash— …GINA!!! RUN FROM THE LIGHT! SOMEONE ELSE IS HERE! RUN! RUN!!"

The beam bounced off the walls like a strobe light and finally stopped when it hit one of us—Gina. She was only inches away from me. I grabbed her arm.

"AGGGH!"

"It's me! Give me your hand!" I yelled, as we bumped into one another. Suddenly, the light went off, and it was pitch black again.

"How are we gonna get out?" she quivered.

"Listen to the sounds. When we hear the oil burner, we'll be close to the bulkhead. But don't say a word till then."

The sweat was soaking my clothes. I tried to shut out the thought that someone else was with us and concentrate on the sounds. My ears were trying to hear above the sound of my own thumping heart. Finally, they picked the droning of the oil burner on my left, and then the up-and-down crashing of the bulkhead door above us. I didn't have to say anything to Gina, all I did was give her hand an extra squeeze. That's when the yellow beam appeared two inches away from us! We're dead, I thought, and froze. But before I could blink the flashlight fell to the floor, followed by a faint "Owww."

"Let's go!" Gina yelled.

We scaled the steps in seconds, and then sprinted for the truck.

When I spotted the truck, I knew we were home free, or so I thought!

"We're stuck!" Gina shouted.

"What do you mean, we're stuck?" I couldn't believe what I was hearing.

"Quick, get out and push," her panicked voice ordered. I didn't waste a second. I leaped out and waded through the thigh-high snow that was behind the truck. She revved the engine, and I pushed as hard as I could. The truck rocked back and forth as the exhaust shot out smoke. It felt like the truck was breaking free when the sound of sirens distracted my pushing and caused me to lose my forward motion and fall back into the snowdrift. As I rose to my feet, I noticed a vehicle parked behind some trees about thirty yards away. Even though only a portion of it was peeking through the trees, it resembled an SUV. The CIA agent who was assigned to follow me, I thought.

"Come on, hurry! The cops are coming," Gina pleaded.

"Hit the gas on three," I shouted while getting a firm grip on the bumper and traction under my footing.

"One. Two. Three!"

The engine raced and the tires squealed while I grunted and pushed and grunted and pushed. The snow suddenly made a crunching sound and I fell face first to the ground—the truck had broken free. Gina kept one hand on the wheel and pushed the passenger door open with the other.

"Come on, Orville, let's hit it!"

She didn't have to yell it twice as I dove into the truck. She shifted into gear and sped off. She must've been driving about fifty miles per hour on the poorly plowed road. We had to drive past Dr. Dowd's house to get out of Old Oyster Road, and as we zoomed past the house I looked over to see if anyone was in the yard.

"Oh no," I heard Gina gasp before the truck swerved out of control and hit the three trash barrels before coming to a stop in the front yard. Trash was scattered all over the drifting snow.

"What happened?"

"Someone ran out in front of the truck." She punched the steering wheel in anger. The sirens were getting closer. I figured Gina would try to start the truck immediately, but she didn't. She was staring out at the trash.

"Gina, any day now."

Gina ignored my sarcasm. "Orville, go grab one of those trash bags."

"What for?"

"I'll explain later." She turned the key and the engine awoke. There must be a logical reason, I figured. So I grabbed the nearest trash bag and threw it into the back of the truck.

"Go. Go," I said, as I jumped back in.

We burned down to the beginning of Old Oyster Road.

"Right or left?" she asked.

I spotted flashes of blue and white lights in the distance on the left. Nothing was on the right.

"Take a right. But I don't know where to go."

"I do." Gina spun the wheel clockwise.

"Where?" I asked.

"You'll see, partner, you'll see." Her eyes concentrated on the winding road. All I could do was wonder what trouble that winding road was leading us to.

Chapter Seven

"I'M TELLING you, this is foolproof. The fortune-teller will touch the trash, and maybe she'll feel a piece that will trigger a vision or something and then we can figure out what this is all about." Gina's eyes danced. We were about ten yards from Hilda's wagon when I stopped walking.

"I don't know if it's a good idea, Gina." I had second thoughts about the plan.

"What do you mean? You said it was brilliant when we were in the truck driving here.

"I know, but I wasn't thinking of Hilda. You see, the last time I asked her to try to have a vision she got very upset. Seeing the pain of someone's past or future bothers her." I tried to make Gina understand.

"Bothers her? And finding Dr. Dowd dead, covered in bees, doesn't bother me? Not to mention the idea of his killer knowing our names and what we look like? Do you think that doesn't bother me? This could be life or death, Orville, so forgive me if I'm insensitive about the fortune-teller's feelings." Gina was furious. I had never seen her like this before.

"I have a name."A voice from behind surprised us.We snapped our heads back and saw Hilda's crouched figure. She was supporting herself with a twisted cane.

"My name is Hilda." She said to Gina.

"I'm sorry. I'm ... I'm ..."Gina was visibly embarrassed.

"Do not be sorry, child.We do not have time for that. Come."

Hilda inched in front of us and headed for the wagon. Gina and I gave baffled looks and then followed.

"You know what to do if I have any customers, Maxwell."Hilda spoke to Maxwell while he held the door open to the wagon.

"Yes, Hilda. No distractions."

Hilda nodded thanks and continued into the wagon.

"Orville, I think by now, you know how to do this." Her eyes narrowed as she took off her coat and hung it up in the corner. I ushered Gina to the crystal-ball table and sat beside her.A minute later, Hilda came into the room, and I noticed something different about her. She wasn't wearing her costume of scarves or the black gypsy gown. Instead, she was wearing a flower-patterned dress and a white pearl necklace. I also spotted lipstick and a touch of blush on her cheeks. If I didn't know her, I would have thought she was heading to a senior citizens' social.

"Gina, I wish I could offer you some tea but it is all gone. Orville and I have drunk quite a bit of it the last few days." She gave a thin smile and settled into her chair.

"Oh, that's OK. I'm fine. I'm sorry about outside, it's just ..."

"There is no need for apologies because for the most

part you were right. Now empty your pockets of the trash."

We did as Hilda requested and put a variety of different objects on the table.

There was an apple core, crumpled pieces of paper, an ace playing card, a postcard from a friend vacationing in Aruba, a book of matches, and a number of other odds and ends.

"Gina figured we should bring you the stuff that Dr. Dowd would have probably touched the longest." I said.

"That was wise thinking," Hilda said before closing her eyes. She picked up the postcard first and held it with her left hand while rubbing it slowly with her right. After a minute of sighing she moved on to the book of matchsticks. Without opening her eyes, she scattered the matches on the table and pressed both her hands on them. "I'm ... I'm ... No ..." She shook her head and like a blind person felt around for the next object—the apple core. She held it firmly in her hand.

"Snowy night. He is ... he is just eating an apple."

The procedure continued with a bottle cap, an electric bill, and a shampoo bottle. With each object the same result—no visions.

We were running out of objects and Gina gave me a this-isn't-working look, which I returned with a grim nod.

"Wait ... wait ... It is not clear ... but I see somesing ...." Hilda said as she held the ace playing card in her right hand. As I waited anxiously, I quickly wondered, Why would anyone throw out one playing card? It didn't make sense.

"Yes ... What is that?" Hilda asked no one in particular, and then rubbed her finger faster along the face side of the card. "I see somesing. It is ..." She stopped and almost crumbled the ace in her hand. "Oh, yes. It is clear now. It is sunny out. It looks like summer. A man is walking onto a ferry. The ferry is carrying cars, too. Not many cars, though. Yes, there are only about six cars on the ferry. The ferry is in or near a harbor because I see many other boats tied up. I cannot make out the man's face. I can only see from his vantage point. He is looking at someone. He gives a quick wave as the ferry begins to move away. I see the other man. He is on the beach. I have seen this man before. He is the man who doesn't have many teeth ... I ... I ... that's it." Hilda opened her eyes.

"It sounds like the car ferry to Chappaquiddick on Martha's Vineyard. If Pushkin is still alive and around here, I bet that's where he's hiding," I exclaimed.

"Yeah, it's gotta be," Gina said, jumping to her feet. "The Vineyard is the only place around here I can think of that has a small car ferry."

"Pushkin is the key to all of this. Alive or dead. At least, that's what my gut is telling me." I was sure.

"Always listen to your instincts, Orville." Hilda handed me the tattered ace. I glanced at it briefly. Ace of diamonds. Maybe our luck is changing. I shoved the card into my back pocket.

"Hilda, thank you so much," Gina said.

"You are welcome, Gina." Hilda paused. "Could you give Orville and me a moment alone?"

"Oh, yeah. Sure," Gina said to Hilda, and then turned to me. "I'll wait outside." She shut the door.

"I like her Orville. Shee's a strong young woman. You will be very lucky to... I wish I could haf... anyway, I just wanted to say good-bye if I do not get to say it later."

"What? I thought the carnival was going to run through next weekend." I was confused.

"It vas originally. Unfortunately, Mr. Coté does not have his father's business skills. A vinter carnival on the Cape Cod is wonderful for four days but after that it is a little too much. So the carnival is packing up the trains tomorrow night and is heading for Canada. Much snow there. So, this is good-bye." Hilda eased out of her chair. As I hugged Hilda good-bye, an unexplainable feeling of emptiness filled me and my eyes began to burn. I was surprised at my emotions considering I hardly knew her. When she let go of me, she wiped her eyes dry and laughed, "I guess, I am fully living."

"Goodbye, Hilda." I forced a smile and turned to open the door.

"Orville, one more thing."

"Yes."

"That hug just gave me a feeling and a vision."

I didn't say a word. I just nodded for her to continue.

"Trust whoever has the daisies and no one else. I am sorry, that is all I felt and saw." I nodded again and headed out of the wagon filled with a strangely familiar feeling of sadness and joy.

Gina and I went to Paul's Pizza, a favorite among Belltowners, to get something to eat but most of all, to catch our breath. The past couple of hours had been wild ones and we really needed to calm down and sort everything out. As we waited for our shrimp pizza, I filled Gina in on where the bees came from.

"So, who told you the bees were stolen?" she asked before sipping on her soda.

"Eve Capshaw. She's a reporter for the *Belltown News*. She said that some beekeeper said that about two thousand of his bees were stolen from his special room."

"Well, we know where they are now." Gina shivered and then said, "But why were they in Dr. Dowd's house and also why were they on his body?"

"I have no clue. The whole thing is pretty weird." I nodded and then took a long sip from my straw.

"Hey, Orville." A voice interrupted us. I looked over from our booth and spotted my buddy Dan "Franco" Francais standing by the cash register.

"Hey, Franco." I waved to him, and he came over holding a stack of five pizza boxes.

"What's up, Orville? Oh, hi Gina." Franco's tone changed when he saw Gina. He seemed almost nervous.

"Hi, Dan." Gina gave a bright smile. I gave her a look. No one ever called Franco by his first name.

"Sit down—join us." I moved over to make room.

"I wish I could, but I just came in to get our pizzas. My Dad's parked outside. Hey, are you guys psyched about tomorrow?"

"What's tomorrow?" We both asked.

"No school. I just heard it on our way over. They're expecting at least eight to twelve inches more," Franco said while looking at Gina.

"Awesome!" Gina and I replied. A moment later, the waitress appeared with our piping-hot shrimp pizza.

"Well, I better get going." Franco paused. "I'm .... Gina, can I talk to you for a minute?"

"Sure, Dan. I'll be right back, Orville." Gina shot out of the booth.

"Later, Franco," I said.

"Yeah, later, Orville."

Gina called Franco "Dan" twice. Something was going on between those two, I thought as I peeled a piece of shrimp off my pizza and chewed it.

A minute later, Gina came back and sat down with a guilty smile on her face.

I mimicked her voice, "Sure, Dan."

"Orville, don't even start," she said, as she reached for a piece of pizza.

"Well, what was that all about?"

"He just wanted to know if I'd like to go sledding tomorrow."

"Really? Are you going to go?"

"I told him I might have plans but I'd call him in the morning."

"Plans? So you don't like Franco?"

"No, I think I do, but we still have to figure out what we're going to do about Pushkin."

"Oh, yeah. I almost forgot." I almost did. I was so stunned that Franco was interested in Gina and vice versa. Franco was a jock and Gina was a free spirit. They were complete opposites. "Well, since there is no school, I'll probably take the eight o'clock boat tomorrow to the Vineyard and then jump on that small car ferry that Hilda was talking about and go to Chappaquiddick and see if I can find where Pushkin is hiding. That is, if he's hiding over there."

"You mean see if *we* can find Pushkin," Gina said before chomping on her pizza.

"I should try talking you out of coming but I know it would be a waste of time, Ace."

"Ace?" Gina didn't understand so I reached into my back pocket and pulled out the tattered ace of diamonds and threw it onto the table.

"Ace is your new nickname, Gina. After all, if you didn't have Hilda touch the trash and this ace of diamonds, we would be at a dead end. Now, we at least have hope."

"Ace. I like that name." Gina wiped her hands with a napkin and then picked up the ace of diamonds and studied it. She seemed transfixed with the card for a while and then she slid her fingernail in one of the bent corners. It looked like she was trying to peel the card apart. Even though I was curious, I didn't say anything. I was too busy munching on my third piece of pizza.

"Oh, man! Orville, look at this." Gina had peeled the top layer with the ace of diamonds insignia right off the card, revealing something else. I hopped over to Gina's side of the table when I saw what she had uncovered. Hidden underneath the top layer of the Ace was a second layer with handwritten words.

"I can't believe this." Gina shook her head.

"I can't either. What's it say?"

"Take E to Ch. half of a dollar trees on L butt twisted

tree oar on floor to the door." Gina looked up. "They're directions, but to where?"

"The first part is a piece of cake," I said, smiling. "Take ferry to Chappaquiddick ..."

"Half a dollar must mean go half a mile and look for the trees on your left." Gina jumped into the figuring.

"Yeah, you're right. What about this butt twisted tree part?" I pointed to the handwriting and we both thought for a moment and then it came to me. "Aw, man, that's easy. Butt is spelled with two t's as in your behind. So behind the twisted tree..."

"There must be an oar on the ground that has the directions to where Pushkin is staying," Gina finished.

"That explains why Hilda had the vision of the car ferry and Chappaquiddick when she touched just this card. Dr. Dowd was most likely carrying it with him when he went over to the Vineyard," I surmised.

"The only problem, it was this summer. The oar with the directions is probably long gone by now." Gina handed me back the part of the card with the directions and I put it away.

"Yeah, you're right. But at least we know we're going to play in the right ballpark." I got up and was about to get back on my side of the table when I noticed Officer Warner at the cash register. He was looking at his takeout number, but then stopped and unclipped the walkie-talkie off his belt. He shouted something into it and spoke quickly to the woman behind the register and then bolted out the door. It was apparent something was wrong so I hurried over to the cash register for an explanation.

"Why did Officer Warner take off like that?" I interrupted the woman behind the register, who was adding up the bill. She looked up. "Huh? I'm, oh, he got a call on his radio." She was preoccupied.

"Do you know what it was about?"

"Yeah, something about someone being in serious condition at the winter carnival." She went back to her adding.

I didn't want to listen to my gut but it was talking and I didn't like what it was saying—Hilda was in trouble.

I was hoping the swirling red and white lights by Hilda's wagon were carnival lights. I quickly realized it was false hope as the red and white lights of the ambulance slowly passed Gina and me and exited out the side gate. The ambulance is going too slow, I thought as I sprinted to the wagon. I pushed my way through the crowd of whisperers and finger-pointers until I came to Maxwell, who sat in the snow with his head buried in his hands.

"Maxwell. What happened?"

He didn't respond.

"It's Hilda, isn't it? What happened to her?" I shouted. He still didn't look up. He just pointed to the wagon door, and I jumped up the two steps as I heard an onlooker say, "The police said not to go in there." I ignored the warning and opened the door. Officers Jameson and Warner had plastic gloves on and they were searching the wagon while Chuck Coté looked on.

There was no sign of Hilda. Officer Jameson saw me first and snapped, "Orville, what are you doing in here?"

"Where's Hilda? What happened to her?"

"You knew her?" Officer Jameson's eyebrow raised.

"Yeah, where is she?" I asked the question because I didn't want to face what I knew.

"Mr. Coté, can you take Orville out of here? We still have some work to do." Officer Jameson gave Chuck a look I could interpret and my eyes began to water. Chuck grabbed my arm.

"Let go of me! Tell me! Tell me how she died . . . Please . . . She was a friend of mine." The tears rolled down my cheeks. Officer Jameson looked at me long and hard and then said, "Warner, can you go outside and control the crowd until we get some backup?" Officer Warner nodded and left.

"Orville, I'm sorry. Hilda died from heart disease," Officer Jameson said sympathetically.

"Oh, no. No. No. No." It was all I could say.

"Orville. Hilda suffered many years and tonight her heart finally gave out." Chuck put his hand on my arm to console me, but it didn't work. I cried for a minute and finally caught my breath, "She knew she was going to die tonight."

"Why do you say that?" Officer Jameson frowned.

"I just know it. I felt a strange sense of loss when I hugged her goodbye, and also the way she was dressed. She was dressed up. She wanted to look good. You know, as though she were going to a dance."

"Maybe she did know, but Orville, take comfort in

the fact that Hilda died in her sleep. She was taking a nap and didn't feel a thing." Chuck pointed to the other room. I opened the drapes that separated the rooms and stared at the empty bed. I felt my jaw quivering again when something caught my eye, something that didn't seem to fit. As I entered Hilda's room, Officer Jameson said, "Orville, you can't go in there."

"Why not?"

"I don't want you to get your fingerprints on anything." As I walked to the object on the nightstand I said, "It should not matter what I touch. You said Hilda died of natural causes."

"Well, yeah. But..." As Jameson searched for an explanation I peered down at the Styrofoam cup on the dresser next to Hilda's bed.

"Whose is this?" I pointed at the cup that was half-filled with coffee.

"It was Hilda's. She must've had it before she took her nap. Now c'mon Orville, let's go outside," Jameson said abruptly.

"Hilda was murdered, wasn't she?" I tried to stay calm but I was boiling. I knew they weren't telling me the truth.

"Orville, that's ridiculous," Chuck Coté said. "Why do you say that?" Jameson didn't even flinch.

"Well, first of all, you're wearing gloves and searching the wagon. And the other reason I say that is because that's not Hilda's Styrofoam cup of coffee."

"How do you know that?" Jameson asked.

"Because Hilda hated coffee. You might want to stop lying to me and find out who murdered my friend." I stormed out of the wagon in anger, pain, and confusion. But there were a couple of things I wasn't confused about. One, my investigating had caused Hilda's death. There would never be a worse feeling than having that burden on my shoulders. The other thing I wasn't confused about was that someone was going to pay and that was a promise I was going to keep—no matter what.

On the ride home, Gina suggested we let the police in on everything we had uncovered. She felt that our information would clearly help them in their investigation of finding Hilda's killer. I told Gina I would do that in a heartbeat if I knew I could trust them, but Hilda had specifically warned me not to trust anyone, except whoever has the daisies. Gina didn't say a word until she pulled into my driveway. "OK, we won't tell anyone yet. What time does the boat to the Vineyard leave tomorrow?"

"Eight."

"I'll be over at seven. Later."

"Later, Gina." I shut the door and watched her truck make tracks until it was out of sight.

I barely had any energy as I opened my door and lumbered into The Shack. I was emotionally drained from the tragedy and I really just wanted to get some sleep, but the red light on my answering machine was blinking. I pressed the button: "Hi, Orville. It's Vanessa. It's ah...quarter of seven. Where are you? Give me a call if you get in before ten." I looked at my watch for the first time that night.

It was 11:49. I hadn't talked to Vanessa since the carnival, and I hoped she didn't think I was playing mind games with her.

Beep.

"Orville, it's Mark. Remember me? Your best friend who summers in Belltown? Return my call, will ya? Later."

"Man, he's gonna kill me when I finally call him," I muttered to myself. Mark had left about six messages in the past couple of weeks, but I hadn't had the time to return his calls.

Beep.

"Orville, Eve Capshaw. We need to talk. You know what about. Call me at 555-1986. ASAP."

Uh, oh, I thought, Eve Capshaw was onto me. There was no way I was going to talk to her.

I pushed the erase button and said, "Sorry Eve. But I'm not going to help you get a byline."

"I don't need your help," a female voice said from inside my closet. The voice startled me. The door opened, and there stood Eve Capshaw in my pile of dirty clothes.

"Boy, you sure have a lot of concert t-shirts," she said nonchalantly.

"How did you get in here?"

"The door was open," she said, while pulling a notebook out of her handbag.

"No, it wasn't," I snapped.

"It was," she said firmly, as she scribbled something quickly onto a piece of paper.

"Eve, what are you doing here?" I decided to stop arguing with her.

"I came to talk to you about that internship at the paper you wanted." She ripped the piece of paper out of the notebook.

"Internship? I ..."

"Well, congratulations, you got it." She made a "sssh" sign with her finger to her mouth and then handed me the piece of paper. It read, *Don't talk. I have reason to believe that the CIA has bugged your place. Let's go outside.*

Eve kept talking. "So, I was in the neighborhood and saw that your lights were on and I thought I'd tell you personally that you got the student internship."

"Well, that's great. I'm so excited." I acted enthusiastic as I pointed to the back door. We slipped out and went about fifty feet when Eve said, "I think it's safe."

"Why do you think the CIA bugged my Shack?"

"My source told me. He called and told me a lot of things. He said that two men went in there about a half hour after you found Dr. Dowd's body. He said they were with the CIA," Eve whispered.

"Dr. Dowd? He's dead?" I acted surprised.

"Orville, don't play dumb. I got to thinking about your little story about extra credit. It just didn't seem right. So I called Mr. Cali and explained why I wrote the obituary the way I did. I brought your name up and he said he had you in class last year. So, why would you be trying to get extra credit for his class this year? I double-checked the article and the message finally popped out—IVAN IS HERE. It was an acrostic poem. I can't believe I didn't notice it before. I used to write those kinds of poems all the time in the fourth grade. Anyway, I went straight to Dowd's but the cruisers were already there. Now they're trying to hush up everything. So what's going on? Do you know where Pushkin is?" She waited for my answer.

"You mean Pushkin's alive?" Again, I faked shock.

"Well, that's what my source says. He says Pushkin is hiding somewhere on the Cape and he is extremely dangerous. He says all of this is a CIA cover-up but he won't say what it's all about."

"Who's your source?"

"You know I wouldn't tell you even if I knew. But I don't know. I've never seen him. He calls me from a pay phone. He wanted me to tell you that the other night while you were sleeping a CIA agent sneaked into your place and planted a tracking device in your coat sleeve. So they can follow you and not be seen."

That would explain how they ended up parked in the woods by Dr. Dowd's house, I thought. I believed every word Eve said but I couldn't let on. "If that were the case, why wouldn't they also plant a bug on me so they could hear what I was saying?"

"Human error. My source says that the agent assigned to watch you didn't take you seriously. He didn't think you could lead them to Pushkin. He realized he made a mistake when you found Dowd's body."

"OK, so they're tracking me right this minute?" I asked, and Eve nodded.

"So they know that I'm in my backyard in the middle of the night freezing my butt off," I said, faking agitation.

"Yes. So can you give me anything for a story? Do you know what this is all about?" Eve raised her mini tape recorder.

"Yes, I do."

"Well, what's it about?" Her eyes lit up.

"Orville Jacques will be starring in the next *Mission Impossible*. Eve, you've got a wild imagination. See you later." I laughed and walked away. I didn't want to be harsh to Eve but I had to. I had no choice. None of this could get out. I wanted to spill my guts out to her and I thought I could trust her, but I wasn't positive. The whole time I was talking with her, I was looking for daisies. Eve Capshaw didn't have any. I had to find the person who had them!

Chapter Eight

"YOU LOOK horrible. Did you get any sleep?" Gina asked as she walked into my Shack.

"Not a wink. How 'bout you, honey?" I said affectionately, and Gina looked at me like I was crazy but said, "A couple of hours but right when I was getting some serious zee's, I got your wakeup call. So what couldn't wait another hour?"

I handed her a piece of paper with the plan I had been working on all night. I gave her a nod to read it. I leaned over and spoke clearly into the penny-sized device that I had found inside the lampshade on my desk. "I couldn't wait another hour to see you, honey. I planned the whole day for us. Breakfast, sledding, and a trip to the museum. What do you say, honey?" Whoever was listening in probably thought I was a sappy boyfriend. At least, that's what I was hoping. I was also hoping Gina would go along with the plan. She finished reading and walked over to the lampshade and said overly sweetly, "Sugar cookie, that sounds like a great plan."

But she wrote on the paper, *What do I tell Dan?* I wrote back, *Tell him the truth.*

I was hesitant to involve Franco Francais in my plan, but I needed a third person to make it work. I had known Franco for years and he was one person who didn't need to have daisies to be trusted.

"Oh, honey before we get breakfast, can you pick up Franco? I promised him that he could use my Shack to study today. He really has to get his grades up if he wants to be eligible to play on the football team next year."

"Anything for you, sugar cookie. I'll be back in a half hour." Gina shut the door. My plan was now in motion.

A half hour later Gina and Franco arrived. Franco was carrying his book bag and he still had bed head. "Hey, Orville, thanks for letting me study in your place. I really need to get those grades up." Franco's acting wasn't exactly going to win an Academy award, but it worked.

"No problem. Anything to help a friend," I said as we exchanged coats. Franco was barely able to squeeze into my coat. He is much bigger than I am, and that was the only part of my plan I was worried about. But I was betting on the fact that with the tracking device in the coat, the CIA agent would keep a safe distance and wouldn't pick up the noticeable size difference. I gave Gina a note that read, *I'll call you guys at Coffee Obsession at 4:00. If you don't hear from me then and only then call the police and tell them everything!*

Gina nodded OK. Franco took the note pad off my desk and wrote, *Orville, I still don't know what this is about. I look stupid in your coat so if this turns out to be some practical joke, I'll make you pay. Franco style!*

"Franco style" is what they called a quarterback who would have to leave a game after Franco sacked him.

I wrote back, *Franco, it's no joke! Gina has all day to tell you what's going on. I hope you don't mind spending the day with her?*

Franco read it and gave me a smile and a slap on the back before they headed outside. I peeked through my curtains and watched the truck drive away. About three minutes passed, and that's when I spotted a blue SUV slowly rolling down the road headed in the same direction as Gina and Franco and of course, my winter coat. My plan had worked—I had lost the CIA agent.

The boat ride to Martha's Vineyard was surprisingly calm considering the Nor'easter we had the previous night. I spent most of the forty-five minute voyage on the deck feeding the seagulls my honey-dipped doughnut while gazing in deep thought at the gray-slate sky. I thought about Eve's source. Could it be a CIA agent? After all, Eve's source had told her that the CIA agent assigned to follow me didn't take me seriously. How would the source know that unless he/she was an agent? And if that were the case, what would a CIA agent gain from warning me? I also thought about how the source described Pushkin as being extremely dangerous. But what I was thinking about most was something Hilda had said when I asked her why she changed her mind and helped me. I went over the words in my mind: "I might not tell you why I changed my mind, but someday I'll let you know. And remember I was smiling when I told you this." Among all the other riddles, I was praying that I would find an answer for that one. The blaring boat horn shook me out of thought and informed me that we were entering Edgartown Harbor. One step closer, I thought, but to what?

My next step was to jump onto the small car ferry to "Chappy"—that's what all the locals called it—but it wasn't as easy as I had anticipated. It took me almost a half hour to find the captain. After searching almost every shop in Edgartown, I finally found him eating breakfast in a Mom-and-Pop type restaurant. He reluctantly pushed his omelet away and confessed with a smile, "I thought I'd take a chance that no one would want to go over to Chappy this morning."

The ferry ride took only about ten minutes, but it seemed like a long ten minutes. The captain was curious about my trip, so I made a quick excuse about wanting to take pictures of the landscape for my photography class. Photography just happened to be his passion, and he told me about different cameras and pictures he had taken. Luckily, we docked before he could ask me what camera I was using—I didn't have one. Next time have your story down, I thought to myself as I walked along the deserted road. I had memorized the directions and spoke them softly to myself. "Half of a mile. Trees on left. Behind twisted tree. Oar on floor to door." The only problem was there were more trees on my left than I had anticipated, and there was no way of marking a half mile. I had to guess. Trial and error. And error was the word. Several times I got off the main road and searched behind the endless forest, but there were no twisted trees. I must have spent close to an hour but I couldn't help it. "It has to be here," I said above the hunger pangs in my stomach. I'd eaten only half a doughnut and my stomach was begging me to open the lunch I had packed. I was about to consider my stomach's request when I spotted another group of trees ahead on the left. I made a deal with myself: if there wasn't a twisted tree in that group, I would eat my bologna-and-cheese sandwich and chips. As I approached the trees, my heartbeat began to rise at what I saw off the main road—fresh footprints leading directly to the trees. I cautiously followed the prints until I came to one lone tree that actually resembled two trees intertwined—a twisted tree! Oh man, this is it! I looked behind the tree and spotted the paddle half of an oar on the ground. Someone must've wiped off the snow to uncover the oar, I thought. I crouched over and noticed that the oar was secured to a piece of metal or something. My eyes searched for the directions on the oar but I couldn't find any. So I tried to pull the oar off the piece of metal it was secured to. The oar only went up halfway but something ten feet in front of me sprang out of the ground sending snow flying. I couldn't believe it. I whispered to myself, "Oar on floor to the door." The oar was actually a trigger to opening a trap door in the ground. I pushed the oar down and the trapdoor slammed back into the ground. I didn't know what to do next—open the trapdoor again and search or come back later with Gina so I'd have a lookout? Deep down, I knew the decision I was going to make, but a voice with a foreign accent came from behind me and eliminated my choices. "Do not move, my friend. I have gun pointed at your head. Do not say word. Pull up oar. Come. I do not have all day. Go down there." The gun pressed into my back, making my trembling body move forward to the opening in the ground.

I looked down. "It's pitch black. What do you want me to do, jump?"

"No. There is rope ladder." The man sounded as nervous as I was.

"Where?" I began to turn to see who he was. It must be Pushkin, I thought.

"I said, do not turn!" He pressed the barrel harder. "I know you can see ladder."

"OK. OK. I see it now. But I have to turn around to climb down."

"Turn slowly and keep your eyes to ground."

I did as he ordered and climbed the twelve-foot rope ladder. I figured he would shut the door behind me, but instead a light flashed down into my eyes as he slowly made his way. I knew this was my chance to jump him because he needed at least one hand to climb, and the other held the flashlight.

I was getting ready to make my move when he said, "If you try to jump me I will turn flashlight off and shoot."

A moment later, the flashlight was level in my eyes. I heard the man pull something, and the trapdoor slammed shut.

"OK, sit. Over there." With the beam, he directed me to a chair. "Look, I am not want to hurt you."

"Yeah, right. I've heard about you, Pushkin," I stammered, my guessing.

"What? What did you say?" the man asked in shock.

"Pushkin, Nicholas Pushkin is your name. And this past summer you fought a man on your boat. He fell overboard and you let him drown. So don't lie to me and say you're not going to hurt me!"

There was silence and with it came beads of sweat on my brow, and a soaring heart rate. I was positive that the silence was telling me that he was going to kill me. Why didn't I play dumb? my mind hollered. Finally, he threw something at me and I flinched and yelled out, "Please, don't kill me!"

"Calm down, they are only matches! Light those candles on table beside you."

My hand shook as I struck a match and lit the six candles in a holder. The room lit up immediately. It was a bare room with concrete walls and a door to another room. I turned to face the man with the gun and my hunch was right. Standing in front of me with a toothless piercing stare was Nicholas Pushkin.

He was dirty and worn. The only thing that looked clean was the small, shiny black gun he waved at me. "Toss me backpack and sit down."

He rummaged with one hand through the pack until he came to my sandwich. "Do you mind? I have not had real food in weeks."

"Yeah, sure," I was able to utter. He kept his eyes on me while he ate the sandwich in seconds. When he finished he said, "Who are you? How do you know my name? How did you know about man on boat? And how did you know how to find me?

"I'm ... my name is Orville Jacques but you won't

believe how I know about the man you let drown."

"I did not let him drown. He fell overboard when he tried to kill me. I tried to save him. But by time I pulled him out he was already dead."

"So then you put your wallet in his pocket so the CIA would think the dead man was you?"

"Yes …Wait …CIA? How do you know about them … this … How do you know? Tell me?" He waved the gun at me.

"Hold on! I don't know much. I just know pieces. Thank God, Joe Clancy never got to know the real Nicholas Pushkin."

"What? Joe Clancy? The little guy who eats ice cream? What does he have to do with this?" He was baffled.

"Joe told me that you were a good man. But you're just a lunatic with a gun!"

Pushkin looked at the gun in his hand and then slowly put it into his coat pocket.

"Look … Orville, that is name, no?"

I nodded, feeling a little relieved. "Yes, Orville Jacques."

"I am not crazy. I am just confused here. You are telling me things you should not know. So could you try to make sense?" Pushkin was firm.

"I found a skeleton of the man who drowned. The police said it was you but I saw the body and the man had all of his teeth. Joe told me about your teeth so I knew it had to be a cover-up especially when I overheard that the CIA was looking into it."

"When did you find body?" There was urgency in his voice.

"I don't know, a couple of days ago. It's one long blur.

Wait—so you haven't seen the *Belltown News?"*

"No. I could only get paper if I went to Edgartown and you probably can tell I have not been out much lately." He looked down at his soiled clothes.

"Well, that's how I tracked you here."

"What do you mean?" He was getting edgy again.

"I read your obit in the paper and found out Dr. Dowd paid for it. I found this in the trash." I pulled out the ace.

"Oh! I told Doctor to burn directions months ago! I am going to kill him when I see him!"

"You're too late."

"What are you talking about?"

"I found Dr. Dowd last night. He was...dead."

"Oh, no. No! No! No! No! Oh, I never should have involved him. He thought it was all some sort of game." Pushkin sat down. He looked defeated and I contemplated making a run for it, but something made me stay.

"Who is Ivan?" I blurted.

"What? What did you say?" His eyes froze in fear.

"The capital letters in the obit formed a message. Ivan is here."

"Ivan is here! Oh, no! No! It is no use now. He will find me and all work will be for nothing." He stared blankly.

"What work? Pushkin, I know you are probably going to kill me, but at least let me die with the knowledge of why!" I was frustrated. I couldn't take it anymore. I felt a large lump form in my throat as he reached into his pocket and pulled out the gun.

"Orville, I am not going to kill you. I could not hurt a fly. You see this Walther PPK, it is not my gun. I got it off that former KGB agent who tried to kill me on boat." He placed the gun on the table, and I looked at it briefly but said, "The KGB, wasn't that the Russian secret police?"

"Yes, they performed the same duties for Russia as CIA performs for America. Ivan Petralkov used to be an agent, but now he has his own company and he and the CIA are after me."

"But why?"

"If I tell you... you could be in...great danger."

"I know. I've already been. There was a man in Dowd's house who knows who I am. It's probably Ivan."

"Did he have shaved head and black mustache?

"I don't know. I didn't get a good look. Does Ivan kill a person and then put bees on their body?"

"Bees?"

"Yes, Dr. Dowd's body was covered with bees."

He thought for a minute. "Oh, yes that makes sense. That cruel ... Yes, Dr. Dowd was allergic to bees and because of it bees were his greatest fear. That is how Ivan kills. He finds out your greatest fear or hate and kills that way. I guess you do deserve to know the truth. My real name is Demetri Bunzl. Up until twelve years ago, I was nuclear chemist in Russia. Three other colleagues and I for many years worked on top-secret projects in an underground facility in Siberia. Twelve years ago, we unfortunately completed one of our toughest assignments just as I was about to resign."

"Why do you say unfortunately completed the assignment?"

"We were assigned to create substance that could be ingested by human being and half hour later cause the person to explode with a force that could take out city block. The substance tasted like salt and all you needed to ingest was about three pinches. It was revolutionary breakthrough. One that people before could only imagine. A body acting as bomb."

"Oh, my God! So you mean people could eat this without knowing and then literally blow up?"

"Yes, imagine what one salt shaker in a restaurant would be capable of doing to place like Belltown."

"How could you create such a ..." The horror of it put me at a loss for words.

"We had one supervisor and she was in charge of total project. We were on a need-to-know basis. We didn't know what we were creating. We worked on many top-secret projects. When we were done, one of my colleagues accidentally found some documents stating what we created and that we succeeded. We were horrified."

"But you were nuclear chemists. What did you expect?"

"You are correct. But something had happened to change all four of us. Anyway, with help of hundred other comrades, we constructed a plan and took over facility. We destroyed all valuable data, and I changed code to the facility. Without code, no one can get in. The one thing we could not destroy was the two tons of Death Powder that were already created.

"So, that's why Ivan and the CIA are after you, they want the code to the facility?"

"That is definitely why Ivan is after me. He wants the code so he can get the Death Powder and sell it on the black market to any chemical terrorist organization who is willing to pay. My government is also after me, and CIA has named the project CODE Z and.... It is last letter in your alphabet. Maybe, having the Death Powder, it will be put on the U.S.'s last line of defense. And having it in any government's hands is chance I do not want to take."

"You mean the U.S. wouldn't destroy it?"

"Maybe and maybe not. That is one too many maybes. And you cannot destroy the Death Powder. If it is not handled correctly it could blow hole in Eastern Europe. That is why I am on Cape. In that other room," he pointed, "I have been working on formula that will safely destroy the Death Powder with no residual effects, just a harmless pink cloud over Siberia for three to five days. I found the missing ingredient a few months ago and I am positive the formula is set."

"But why the Cape?"

"I needed a type of algae that could only be found in your waters. One that only a few of your scientists know about like Dr. Dowd. It is far too complicated to explain. But, that is why I built this underground lab and included Dr. Dowd. He is . . . *was* the premier oceanographer. He also had ties to some of my comrades."

"OK, but I don't get something you said a minute ago about something that happened that made you want to stop creating the Death Powder." I was still skeptical. I had listened to everything he had told me but that didn't mean I believed him. Not in the least.

"April 26, 1986, is what happened. Did you ever hear of Chernobyl Nuclear Plant disaster?" He was deep in thought.

"Yes, I vaguely remember my history teacher mentioning it. There was an explosion in the plant and then radioactive clouds and people died or got cancer and died."

"My three colleagues and I all lost loved ones. I lost my whole life. You see, you have the Atlantic Ocean for front yard. My family had Chernobyl. Since I was a nuclear chemist my government made my family live there. They thought it was good way of showing people that they had nothing to fear. So while I was underground in Siberia working on top-secret projects like nuclear warheads or Death Powder, my son, a firefighter, who wanted simple life, was dying from radiation burns. And then my wife got cancer and died. Now I have cancer. That is why my hair and teeth have fallen out. I do not wear false teeth for reason. It is reminder when I look in mirror of the terrible irony my life has been." Tears rolled down his cheeks as he pulled out a picture and stared at it and handed it to me.

"That's my wife, my son, and me years ago. The happy years. That is why I am doing this, Orville."

I looked down at the faded picture of the three, smiling faces.

"Your wife was very beautiful. What is that she's wearing in her hair?"

"Daisies. That was favorite flower. In the spring she'd always wear them in hair."

Daisies! Trust whoever has daisies and no one else.

I knew what I had to do.

I smiled. "Demetri, there's a bag of potato chips in my pack. You better eat up if you want to have your energy for the trip."

"Trip? What trip? I am not going anywhere, Orville. Dr. Dowd was going to sneak me off Cape and now . . .

"And, now, Demetri, that's my job."

Chapter Nine

FOR THE NEXT twenty minutes I tried to convince Demetri to let me help him escape off the Cape, but he continuously shunned the idea. Then I told him about Hilda's role and how she died because of it.

"You see, Demetri, it's fate that brought me here to help you."

"Fate, huh?" He scratched the stubble on his chin.

"We are similar. I feel the same way about Hilda's death as you probably feel about Dr. Dowd's."

He looked up. "You mean responsible?"

"Exactly. I know by trying to help you I might end up dead, and that really scares me. It really does. But what scares me even more is if I go back to Belltown and forget about all of this. Because you and I both know I won't forget about it. And then I would not only have the knowledge that I was responsible for Hilda's death; I would have the knowledge that I didn't do anything and that Hilda died for no reason at all. Demetri, let me help. Don't let Dr. Dowd's and Hilda's deaths be in vain."

Demetri thought for a minute and then said, "Orville,

you're right. But what can you do?"

"Is there anyone I can contact?"

"No one around here. If I could only get to safe house. Orville, do you have boat?"

"No, I don't. Where's the safe house?"

"Off coast of Maine. What about your friends? Do any of them have boats?" Demetri rushed.

"All of their boats are out of the water till spring. The ferries and fishing boats are the only boats in the water right now." Demetri's eyes lit up. "Of course! Of course! I know fisherman, one I can trust. Positive he would help." He laughed, "He might drop dead when he sees his old buddy Radar still alive. He's the one who gave me nickname."

"Why 'Radar'?" It was a question I wanted to ask before.

"I went fishing with him one day and I caught a lot of striped bass. He said I must have radar. I don't know why he thought I had radar, he was the one who showed me where to fish." There was a wide smile on Demetri's face and a sound of hope in his voice.

"What's the fisherman's name?"

"Clarence Bedford. His boat is docked in Belltown Harbor."

"Clarence Bedford!" I exclaimed. It was fate. A week or so earlier, while I was working on a case, Clarence Bedford had saved my life.

"Yes, that's his name. Do you know him, Orville?"

"Well enough to know that he's an angel in disguise." I smiled.

But Demetri's smile vanished, "The only problem will be the docks. I bet CIA has agents watching those docks at night like hawks. And that's when I would have to leave—tonight."

"So, they'll probably just think Clarence is going out to fish."

"I hope so, but Clarence always comes back from fishing at night. He never goes out then. If CIA has done their homework they'll know that, and they'll also know that Clarence and I are friends. But it's our only chance. Let's just hope they haven't done their homework."

Demetri put out his hand and I shook it.

"Yeah, let's hope." I bit my lip. Part of me wanted to tell him what I was thinking, but the other part knew I shouldn't. I had a plan. If it worked no one would be watching the docks and Demetri and the formula would be safe. If it didn't work, nobody would be safe.

I took the 2:15 boat back to Belltown, and as the boat entered the harbor, I glanced at my watch: 2:45. I had just enough time to go to my Shack, pick up Franco's jacket, and then head over to Coffee 0. But as the boat was docking, I remembered that Clarence Bedford's boat slip was to my left. I checked and then double-checked: no fishing boat.

"Ah, man," I said to myself. Demetri and I knew his escape hinged on a lot of ifs, but we never took into account the major if. What if Clarence was out at sea fishing more than one day? Then what? I knew I had to find out when Clarence would be back before going any further with my plan. I spotted a fishing boat docked in the slip to my right. There was a tall man standing on the dock hosing the boat down. He was wearing a fish-stained New England Patriots sweatshirt, jeans, and a Red Sox baseball hat.

Perfect, I thought, typical fisherman. He'll know how long Clarence is out.

"Excuse me, sir?" The man jumped a bit when he saw me.

"Oh, ah. Sorry, you surprised me," he said, and turned off the hose. I'm just hosing the boat down." He seemed nervous.

"Yeah, I see. Did you just get back?" I figured I'd have some small talk before I asked about Clarence.

"Yeah, we just got back a little while ago," he said a little louder, and another man surfaced. He was wearing the same type of sweatshirt but his hat was different—a Boston Bruins hat. They both were cleanly shaven, which I thought was odd for fishermen.

"Catch much?" I asked, and they looked at each other.

"Yeah, a bunch off Nantucket," the man in the Bruins hat answered, smiling.

"Really. What did you catch?" I couldn't explain it, but something didn't seem right about the men.

"I'm . . . all different kinds. Y'know." The man in the Red Sox hat turned his hose back on.

I was about to ask about Clarence when the Bruins hat added, "Mostly bluefish. We caught a school of thirty or so."

A school of bluefish, I mused. Bluefish are out of season. There was no way you could find a school of blues in the ocean this time of year. It clicked! They tried to look the part but I didn't buy it. I knew. They were there to keep Clarence Bedford under surveillance. I figured Clarence must be coming back or they wouldn't be wasting their time.

"Blues, huh?" I tried to sound interested.

"Yeah, blues. So what do you want?" I think the man wearing the Red Sox hat knew I was onto them. Then I placed his voice: the agent who made the comment to Officer Jameson about being a small-town cop.

"I was just wondering if you guys need any help on the weekends. I could use a job."

"We're all set." The man in the Sox hat stopped as he watched Clarence's boat enter the harbor and then turned back to me. "Is that it?"

"That's it," I smiled. "Good luck fishing." I finished the sentence in my mind: "Because you're going to need it."

After that encounter, I figured I'd forget Franco's jacket and go straight to Coffee O. After all, the two agents probably radioed to whoever was supposed to have me under surveillance and broke the bad news. I went into Coffee 0 the back way, and spotted Franco and Gina before they saw me. They both had pensive expressions as they watched the ringing telephone. The owner behind the counter answered, "Good afternoon, Coffee Obsession. This is Hugh speaking."

"Is it Orville?" They both jumped. Hugh shook his head "no."

"Man, I don't know if it was a good idea to let him go

on his own," Franco said before chomping on his muffin.

"Well, I see being worried hasn't hurt your appetite," I laughed. "Orville!" they both shouted. Franco pulled a chair over to the table, and I sat down.

"So, what happened?" Gina whispered, excitement in her eyes. "Yeah, did you find anything out?" Franco added.

"Everything," I whispered, and then shouted "Hey, Hugh, can you turn this song up?"

"Sure. No problem, Orville." He turned up the music and I knew we were free of eavesdroppers.

"And can I get a hot chocolate and one of those muffins Franco's got?"

"Don't any of you guys ever order coffee? We have the best coffee on the Cape, y'know." Hugh shook his head and went to work.

"Before I tell you guys, did anyone come in here while you were waiting for me? Say about twenty minutes ago?"

"I told you, Gina," Franco blurted.

"Told her what?" I asked.

"A blond-haired guy, medium build, ran in here about fifteen minutes ago. He looked at Gina and me, and then cursed to himself and ran out. I told Gina, I bet that's the guy who's supposed to be watching Orville."

"Well, Franco, you were right. What about anyone else? Any other strange encounters today?"

I was thinking about Ivan's description—shaved head, black mustache.

They looked at each other and then said, "No."

"Good."

"Wait, there was that one guy. He was kind of strange," Gina said to Franco.

"You mean the guy in the art gallery?" Franco asked back.

"Yeah," she nodded.

"Gina, that guy was an artist. Most of those creative types are a little strange," Franco said, and went back to his muffin.

"Yeah, but I thought that survey was really weird," Gina said.

"What survey? What guy? What'd he look like?" I hoped my questions would break up their banter.

"This guy was in his late fifties, early sixties, and he asked us to take a survey for a painting he was going to work on."

"What color hair did he have?"

"He didn't. His head was shaved, and he had a black mustache."

"And he was foreign. He had an accent like he was German or something."

"Russian," is all I could say.

"Yeah, it could have been. Is he involved in any of this?" Gina asked.

"More than you want to know." I stopped for a minute as Hugh brought me my hot chocolate and muffin. I didn't want to ask the next question but I had to. "What was the survey about?"

Gina and Franco looked at each other for a while and Gina finally answered, "He's doing a painting and he wants the theme to be on a person's greatest fear."

"Greatest fear!" I almost dropped my mug.

"Yeah, he asked us to write down our name and in

what way we fear dying most. He also asked us to do the same for our family and friends, and whoever's name he chose would get a free print of his painting. What's wrong, Orville?" Gina and Franco sensed they had made a huge mistake.

"Did you put down my name?" They both nodded "yes."

"Oh, man," I said in disgust and then asked, "What did you put as my greatest fear?"

"I wrote fear of heights," Franco said.

"I wrote drowning." Gina gave me an "I'm sorry" shrug.

In the past, they would both be right. But I had a new fear, one that was much worse than both of those combined—IVAN.

Gina and I sat in my Shack silently writing notes to one another trying to kill time.

Are you sure Ivan won't follow Dan or hurt him? she wrote, and waited for my response.

If Ivan thinks I've found Demetri, I doubt he would think I would tell Franco, never mind involve him in a plan, I wrote back. Franco's role in the plan was to give Clarence Bedford the message from Demetri.

"But," Gina said and began to write until my clock radio sounded: 6:15.

"OK, it's now or never," I whispered, and went over to the phone and dialed 555-1986.

"Eve Capshaw, what can I ..."

"Eve, Orville Jacques, you still want that byline?"

"Orville, let me get a pen," Eve rushed.

"It's pretty simple. Be at Ferris Gravel and Sand in an hour."

"That's a big place. Where?"

"At the gravel pits."

"But ..." she began. I hung up.

"One down." I looked at Gina and dialed again.

"Belltown Police Department, may I ..." The officer began.

"I have to talk to the CIA agent who is in charge of the Nicholas Pushkin case."

There was a pause on the other end of the line. "Is this some sort of joke?"

"You know what I'm talking about. I need to talk to the head man or woman right now," I ordered.

"Look, our department doesn't have time for games so ... "

"This is no game! Listen to me. I know about Code Z. And I know Nicholas Pushkin is really Demetri Bunzl so you can tell ..."

"Hello, who is this?" another voice asked.

"This is Orville Jacques. Who are you?"

"Special Agent Richard Palmer with the CIA. Orville, we need to talk." His voice was crisp.

"Special agent? Does that mean you have special powers, Agent Palmer?"

"What do you mean?"

"I mean is there a reward for finding Demetri Bunzl and your precious Code Z?"

"Yes, a hundred thousand? Where is he?"

"A hundred thousand," I smiled at Gina before continuing. "Make it a hundred and fifty and it's a deal." I figured I'd at least have some fun.

"Jacques, this isn't a game!" he snapped.

"It certainly is and I've got all the cards. Bunzl and the code to the Death Powder."

There was silence for a minute, "OK, a hundred and fifty. Now where is he?"

"Meet me at Ferris Gravel and Sand in an hour. Oh, and Special Agent Palmer, bring those two clowns I met on that fishing boat today."

"Why?"

"You're going to need all the men you can get to dig."

"Dig?"

"You'll see." I hung up and gave Gina a half-smile and prayed that I wasn't digging a hole I couldn't get out of.

Chapter
Ten

THE TRUCK'S HIGH beams lit up the endless piles of snow-covered gravel and sand. With the snow as a camouflage, the area could have easily been mistaken for the picturesque Montana landscape and not one of the largest gravel pits on Cape Cod. "If you could park here, Gina," I pointed beside a mountain of gravel on our left, "I don't think we'll have to wait long." Gina turned off the engine and we sat in silence for only about ten seconds. Then, headlights blinded us from all sides. "OK, Jacques, you and Miss Goldman please get out of the truck." It was the voice of Special Agent Palmer.

"Wow, you're not the only one wanted in this town." Gina was trying to keep the moment light, but I knew she was nervous. I jumped out and I knew I had to act the same way I did on the phone—cocky.

"All right. Enough with the headlights." I put my hands up to block the blinding beams.

"OK. Turn them off," Agent Palmer ordered, and then walked over to us. My image of him before was that he would be a tall middle-aged type wearing a trench coat like in the movies. In reality, he was probably not even thirty, 5'10", with black hair.

"What was all this talk about shovels?"

"Well, Agent Palmer," I began, as I noticed there were about fifteen to twenty agents carrying shovels. My eyes searched for the two wannabe fishermen and sports fans.

"Well, what?" he asked.

"Well . . ." I stopped for a second and smiled when I spotted the two glaring faces of the fishermen agents. Franco was delivering the message to Clarence and the dock was clear!

I continued, "Well, if you want to find Code Z you're going to have to dig for it."

"Jacques, stop talking in riddles."

"I'm sorry Agent Palmer, it's very simple. You had one of your agents following me around. Well, I found the tracking device in my coat. So I asked my friend to wear the coat. Of course, I made up some story so he would wear it, but we won't get into that." I was going to stall as long as I could.

"No, we won't get into that. Get to the point, will you? We don't have all night." Palmer was obviously agitated.

"OK, OK. Well, during the time you weren't following me, I decided to act on a tip from an unknown source. They told me that Pushkin a.k.a. Demetri Bunzl was hiding out in the gravel pits. So, I came here today and sure enough I found him. I told him I was going to turn him in and that's when it all happened." I paused. More stalling.

"What happened?"

"He begged me not to turn him in. He told me about Code Z and the Death Powder and with the help of Dr. Dowd, he was trying to make some formula to destroy it. He even showed me the code. He had it written between the layers of a playing card. Of course, it was in Russian, so I couldn't read it. But he swore it was genuine."

"He does know," one of the agents blurted.

"Sssh. Go on," Palmer said.

"Well, I told him that I didn't trust him. But deep down, I didn't care, I knew there was probably a reward. Well anyway, he ran over to that area," I said as I randomly pointed to one of the mountains of gravel, "and he fell to the bottom causing an avalanche of gravel that covered him. So he's under one of those piles of gravel."

"Which one?"

"I think it might be that one," I said, pointing to the middle mound, "but I'm really not sure of…"

"What do you mean you're not sure?"

"I mean I'm not sure. I was pretty shaken up at the time."

Agent Palmer turned. "Get Bart Ferris, the owner of this place, on the phone. We need more than shovels to dig Pushkin, I mean, Bunzl up."

"So Nicholas Pushkin wasn't the man they found off of Breakers Beach?" Eve Capshaw came out of the shadows.

"Who the…" Agent Palmer began.

"Eve Capshaw, *Belltown News*."

"Did you call her?" Agent Palmer narrowed his eyes.

I was about to say no when a blond-haired male agent

walked up to Palmer and whispered in his ear. Palmer's face reddened as he turned back to the agent. "He called her five minutes before us, and I'm just finding out about it! Jacques, why did you inform Miss Capshaw? You know this can't get into the paper."

"Why not?" Eve began.

"It's a matter of national security."

I got serious for the first time in a while. I was going to be truthful with Agent Palmer. "I have reason to believe that Miss Capshaw's source is Ivan Petralkov and he might have someone in the CIA working for him."

"Ivan Petralkov! How did ..." Agent Palmer was interrupted by the sound of distant gunshots and then a crackly voice on his radio. "This is Agent Stack. I'm getting shot at near the sand pits on the east side."

"Let's go!" Palmer shouted, and the agents fanned off in different directions.

Eve began to follow.

"Eve, what are you doing? You could get shot!"

"You think I'm going to miss a story because of that?" She took off, leaving Gina and me all alone.

More shots rang out.

"Is it Ivan?" Gina's voice trembled.

"It's gotta be." I looked up and suddenly saw a figure silhouetted by the moon on the top of the gravel mountain to our left. He raised a gun and aimed.

"Gina, watch out!" I pushed her to the ground and a whizzing sound went by my ear. We bounced to our feet.

"Run, Gina! Run!" I yelled, and she began to make tracks, but for some reason I was slowing down. There was a strange sensation in my left leg. My immediate thought was, I've been shot. But it wasn't painful. It was more tingling. My eyes were feeling heavy. I had to have been shot, I figured, so I looked down at my left leg for blood—there wasn't any. I did see something sticking out of my leg and reached to get a closer look but stumbled and fell to the ground. My vision was fading, and the figure was coming closer. I finally pulled whatever it was out of my leg. It felt like pulling out a painful splinter, but a hundred times worse. I studied the feathery needle-shaped object and just when I realized it was a dart, everything went black.

Was I asleep? I wasn't sure. Everything was foggy except the sounds, distant sounds of a moaning fog horn and clanging buoys. Was I at the Belltown Harbor? Why can't I see? I wondered. I knew I was shivering. But why?

"Come on. Wake up!" the voice barked and then somebody shook me out of my groggy state. I rubbed my eyes and my sight was slowly coming back into focus. I was outside, but I wasn't at the gravel pits. A man helped me to my feet. He had a black mustache and a shaved head. I had never seen him before, but I knew him.

"Stand right there."

My legs wobbled for a minute, but then steadied. I focused on the night sky. It was sleeting and raw, and then I looked back at the man. When I spotted the gun in his hand, the headrush of fright returned. "Ivan!"

The man laughed, obviously enjoying my horrified reaction, "Yes, Mr. Jacques. Now where is comrade Demetri Bunzl really hiding?"

"Where am I?" My eyes raced to my feet and hands—they were bound with rope. But, there was something else attached around my ankles. I studied it.

"Those are weights."

"Weights?"

"That is to help you, Mr. Jacques."

"Help me?"

"With your fear of drowning, this way you'll sink to the bottom of the ocean faster and the struggle won't be that long. It is my gift of mercy to you."

"Somebody help!" I yelled at the top of my lungs.

"Ha, ha, ha, ha!" He shook his head. "You really do not know where we are, do you?" He flicked his flashlight on and directed it at the fog beneath us.

"Too much fog below to show you," he yelled above the shrieking wind, and then pointed the light down behind him. I could make out railroad tracks. The reaction on my face must have told him I still didn't know.

"I think this will help you figure things out." He slowly moved the flashlight up from the tracks to the massive iron structure.

"Oh no. No!" I almost fainted out of dizziness when I realized I was standing on the railroad bridge spanning the Cape Cod Canal.

"Your friends told me you were afraid of drowning and heights. I couldn't make up my mind." He looked over the edge with his flashlight. "I wish it was not so foggy. On a clear night, that four-hundred-foot drop is quite a view. Yes," he laughed, "quite a view."

There was a sharp pain in my chest, and the dizziness worsened. I was seeing double, and a second later I collapsed onto the iron surface. He grabbed me around my neck and dragged my limp body near the edge of the bridge.

Then Ivan pointed his flashlight down and whispered in my ear, "Beyond that fog is your grave for eternity. In a few months, your glasses will become sea glass. And I don't have to tell you what you will look like. You have seen that. Just tell me where Bunzl is hiding and I will let you live."

"Why ... do ... you ... think ... I ... know? How ... could ... I ..."

"The fortune-teller. I don't know how, but she helped you."

"And ... you ... killed ... Hilda."

"No, I did not. I was going to but I found her and she had already died in her sleep. I left the half cup of coffee to send you a message. But you did not get it, Jacques, did you! You were supposed to get scared and go to CIA Agent Stack and tell him what you knew."

"He works for you?" Agent Stack, my mind thought, he was the one who shouted about gunshots on the radio. It was just a distraction to get me alone, I realized. There was a feeling of relief that Hilda did die of natural causes and that I made the right decision in not going to the CIA. It all broke through my petrified state and as a result I gave a faint smile.

"I ask the questions!" He leaned down and yelled into

my ear. "Where did you go today? I know it wasn't the gravel pits."

"I'll . . . tell you. I promise. I don't want to die. But... first you have to answer some questions." I had to stall and think of a plan.

"Kid, you have guts." He picked me up and brought me closer to the bridge, removed my glasses and put them into my coat pocket. Why didn't you wear the coat with the tracking device, my mind yelled.

"OK, one question."

"Why didn't you follow me today?"

"That idiot Stack was supposed to follow you. He really thought you believed Miss Capshaw when she told you about the tracking device." He thought out loud. "That's the last time I have that fool work for me."

"So, you were Eve Capshaw's source?"

"Of course. A new reporter like that, if she ever found anything out, I could have dangled her like a puppet. Now Mr. Jacques, where is Bunzl?"

"I don't know."

"You know that's not good enough. Good-bye."

He reached over and pushed me forward. I teetered on the edge briefly and suddenly fog surrounded me and that's when the absolute horror struck. I was falling to my death! I broke through the fog and my blurry vision was able to see the ocean hundreds and hundreds of feet below but approaching quickly. In that split second, my life literally passed before my eyes like a VCR on fast-forward: I saw birthdays, playing ball with my Dad and brother, faces of loved ones young and old. Even though I was going to

die in a couple of seconds, I had a strange feeling of seren-
ity.

Just as I was accepting death, I came to a stop in mid-
air and sprang back up towards the bridge. I looked be-
hind trying to put it all together and that's when I noticed
there was a bungee cord strapped around my feet with
the weights. I was baffled and gasping hard for breath
while being pulled back up to the top of the bridge.

"Did you have fun?" Ivan asked as he heaved me back
up onto the bridge.

"What ... what ... was ..." I tried forming the sentence
but I couldn't. My breathing was labored. I thought I would
choke. I needed air. I inhaled and exhaled in short gasps
until my breathing became natural.

"Well, Mr. Jacques. You just overcame one fear, your
fear of heights."

"You're ... you're ... crazy ... You're beyond crazy!!"

Ivan chuckled. "That's what Dr. Dowd said. Why is it
that dying people always say the same trite phrases?"

"Why didn't you ... just ... kill me? Why this?" I wiped
the sweat off my face and then got sick to my stomach.
My face felt hot and I had trouble focusing.

Ivan ignored me. "Back in Mother Russia when I was
little boy, I had cat. My cat would love to catch the mouse
and play with it, tormenting it for hours. I loved watching
the excitement in her eyes, but after several hours she
would finally kill the mouse or it would escape and her
fun would be over. My fun is not finished yet. Mr. Jacques,
you are my little mouse. Are you going to be a dead mouse
like Dr. Dowd or do you want to live? Your choice." He

took the bungee cord off and replaced it with another—it was shorter. I didn't understand, but I knew whatever the reason, I was in trouble.

"I don't want to die. Please ... please ... look, Demetri Bunzl was hiding in the woods where the winter carnival was held. And the fortune-teller found him and decided to help him. She hid him in one of the tents. You gotta believe me," I begged. Ivan thought for a minute as a loud whistle sounded—a train whistle.

"Really? That is the truth?" He raised his eyebrows. "I can't believe my luck." He smiled.

"What?"

"That train heading this way is Coté's Winter Carnival."

"How do you know that?" I asked, trembling.

"I planned your death that way and now I can jump onto the train and find Bunzl. It would be the perfect way for him to escape."

"What do you mean you planned my death this way? I thought you were going to let me live!"

He laughed. "Never trust crazy man. You see, when train comes to canal, bridge will be mechanically lowered four hundred feet. The tracks will connect and train will ride over canal."

"I know that! I've lived on the Cape all my life. What's your point!" I was burning.

"Shut up, Jacques. As always bridge will only be about thirty feet above canal. Cord I just fit you with is thirty-five feet. My point is, when bridge goes down to the water, it will slowly lower you to a watery grave. You have escaped drowning more than once, but this time you will not."

"How did you know that?"

Ivan howled with laughter. "If I told you, you would die of shock." His strong hands pulled me toward him. His hot breath was in my face. My feet swayed on the narrow steel platform. With one hand he held on to an overhead beam and with his other he pulled me even closer. My feet slipped and I went to my knees, but he held firm to my coat and pulled me up to a standing position. I felt secure for a moment until suddenly he released his grip and shoved me off the platform propelling me into the misty night. I dangled thirty-five feet below the bridge. There was a thunderous noise, and I knew what it was— it was the train bridge slowly lowering the tracks and me. At first, my upside-down view of the ocean was a few hundred feet away and then it was only a few feet away and then mere inches. My eyes bulged and I held my breath as I struggled to break free of the rope.

"Orville, are you OK?" the voice yelled at me. I coughed and looked around. I was lying on the dirt path by the train bridge. There were colored lights swirling and activity all around. Two paramedics hovered over me as Agent Palmer and Gina looked down.

"How did I get here?"

"That guy parachuted out of a chopper, cut you loose, and swam to shore while holding you and fighting the current. He saved your life." He pointed over and I raised my head to see Chuck Coté drinking a cup of coffee.

"How long have I been out?"

"You've been in and out for a half hour."

"Oh, no. Ivan! He's on the train."

"We know. You told us. We got him." Palmer said.

"You did?" I couldn't believe it. "Where is he?"

"One of our agents drove him to our headquarters for questioning about fifteen minutes ago. There's a big reward for his capture that will be yours. As for Bunzl, we can't find him in the pits. And the owner of the pit says it could take a long time but at ...

"Wait a minute! One of your agents took Ivan? It wasn't Agent Stack , was it?"

"Yes, it was Stack. Why?"

"Agent Palmer, forget the reward. Stack is an accomplice. They're both gone."

After three days of being grounded, Mom let me go out with Vanessa. We didn't really "go out" as in a date. I had to take Ophelia for a walk and Vanessa tagged along. I got lost in thought as we stood on the jetties at Breakers Beach. I thought about what Chuck Coté had told me. He received a telegram just as his chopper was leaving:

Orville Jacques—drowning near trainbridge
Cape Cod Canal. Save him. Tell him I changed
my mind because we saved thousands of lives.
I'm smiling—Hilda.

The telegram had been paid for in advance with the strict instructions not to be delivered until Chuck Coté was leaving the Cape. I also thought about Ivan and Demetri. Would Ivan find Demetri in Maine before he could get back to Russia and use the formula? I was upset that I didn't keep my promise to catch Ivan Petralkov.

"What are you thinking about?" Vanessa asked, and moved closer to me. I stared into her eyes and forgot about everything else. "I was thinking that ..." I really wanted to ask to kiss her but I froze in nervousness. We both moved our faces toward each other.

"Did you see that? Jedi, did you see that?"

I couldn't believe it. Joe Clancy came out of nowhere and interrupted our moment.

"What?" I asked, dejected.

"A UFO. I just saw a UFO. Larry, the homeless man, told me he sees them all the time, Jedi. He was right! He was right!"

"Joe, you're crazy." Vanessa laughed.

I stared into the clear night sky and smiled. "Maybe he is, and maybe he's not."

After what I had been through, I was open to believing in just about anything!

EPILOGUE

Two weeks later, a smiling man with a shaved head and a black mustache walked into a coffee shop in a little town on the rocky coast of Maine. He ordered a cup of coffee and unfolded the paper. The smile faded as he read the headline: "Strange Pink Cloud Seen Over Siberia." Ivan Petralkov pounded his fist on the counter. He knew Demetri Bunzl's formula had succeeded in destroying the Death Powder. But all he could mumble as he stormed out of the shop was, "Someday, I'll make that kid pay. Someday!"

About the Author

T. M. Murphy lives in Falmouth, Massachusetts. When he is not writing or cheering for the Boston Red Sox, Mr. Murphy enjoys teaching creative writing to young people. He lives and teaches his Just Write It class in a converted garage he calls The Shack.